AMAZONS: *A Study in Athenian Mythmaking*

AMAZONS

A Study in Athenian Mythmaking

Wm. Blake Tyrrell

THE JOHNS HOPKINS UNIVERSITY PRESS
Baltimore and London

Title-page and chapter-opening ornament: Two types of Amazon armor. Redrawn from an Attic red-figure cup painting, Museo Nazionale, Naples.

Originally published, 1984
Second printing, 1986

The Johns Hopkins University Press, 701 West 40th Street
Baltimore, Maryland 21211
The Johns Hopkins Press Ltd., London

Library of Congress Cataloging in Publication Data

Tyrell, William Blake.
Amazons, a study in Athenian mythmaking.

Bibliography: pp. 155–59.
Includes index.
1. Amazons. 2. Mythology, Greek. 3. Athens (Greece)—
Social life and customs. 4. Matriarchy. 5. Patriarchy.
6. Androgyny (Psychology). 7. Marriage—Mythology.
I. Title.
BL820.A6T95 1984 305.3 83-18782
ISBN 0-8018-3118-0

For Frieda
τῆς φιλίας ἔνεκα

ἡμεῖς μὲν τοξεύομέν τε καὶ ἀκοντίζομεν καὶ
ἱππαζόμεθα, ἔργα δὲ γυναικήια οὐκ ἐμάθομεν.

We practice the bow and javelin and ride horses.
We are not acquainted with women's work.

Herodotus 4.114.3

τοῦτο γὰρ ὅμοιον, ὡς ἂν εἴ τις λέγοι, τοὺς μὲν ἄνδρας
γυναῖκας γεγονέναι τοὺς τότε, τὰς δὲ γυναῖκας ἄνδρας.

This is tantamount to saying that the men of
that day were women, and the women were men.

Strabo 11.5.3

Contents

Preface

THE MANNER OF mythmaking discussed in this book has been and remains a powerful conception of the sexes and of their roles in marriage and in every sphere of life. For  that reason I have tried to keep my study of the Amazon myth from being confined to classicists and other specialists. This has necessitated compromises in depth and extent of treatment whose validity and success must be judged from the finished product. My examination of Aeschylus's *Oresteia* is intended only as a guide to understanding the dynamics of Athenian mythmaking. Works cited once have been given their complete bibliographical reference in the notes. Greek words have been transliterated into their most recognizable form, and all translations are my own. Abbreviations in the notes follow those of N. G. L. Hammond and H. H. Scullard, eds., *The Oxford Classical Dictionary*, 2nd ed. (Oxford: Oxford University Press, 1970).

I am especially indebted to the writings of Jean-Pierre Vernant. I have benefited from conversations about Amazons and mythmaking with Professor Bruce K. Omundson of Lansing Community College and with Larry Joe Bennett, to whom is owed the observation in Chapter Four concerning Amazon liminality in spatial terms. I wish to thank Professor Michael S. Koppisch, of Michigan

State University, for his careful reading of the complete manuscript, and Penny Moudrianakis, of the Johns Hopkins University Press, for her thoughtful improvements and skillful editing. The manuscript has also been improved by the suggestions of my wife, Mary Ann, and by my colleague and friend Professor Frieda S. Brown of Michigan State University. The dedication of this book is intended as a token of my debt and gratitude.

Introduction

PREVIOUS STUDIES of the Amazon myth have very often approached the Amazon as a problem of "myth" or "reality."

Scholars have sought to determine
whether or not Amazons existed and,
if not, what people or peoples inspired
the myth.[1] My reading of the myth
begins with the observation that there
is no way, through modern historical
methods, to affirm or deny the Amazons' existence, since the evidence
we have pertains only to myth and
not to the Amazons *qua* Amazons. Nor is there any profit in
rehearsing theories of their origin, for such theories add nothing
to an understanding of the myth in the classical period. The
existence of the Amazons remains moot. On the other hand, the
myth as a historical product of Greek thought is susceptible to
investigation. This study concentrates upon the meaning of the
myth for classical Athens and has two aims.

The first is to demonstrate that the myth is fabricated from cultural data concerning such matters as war, sex, ethnography, politics, and, above all, rites effecting the transition from socially
defined infancy to adulthood and marriage. Classical Athens was a
patriarchy, a social system organized along the lines of the sexual
asymmetry of male privilege. The cultural ideal, the adult male

warrior, depended upon the imperative that boys become warriors and fathers, and girls become wives and mothers of sons. The genesis of the Amazon myth is the reversal of that imperative: Amazons go to war and refuse to become mothers of sons.

The second aim is to put the Amazon myth into the context of Athenian mythmaking concerning marriage. The Amazon myth explains why it is necessary for the daughter to marry by creating a scenario of the dangers inherent in her not marrying. Moreover, since the myth is part of a larger discourse on marriage as a structure of order among men and as a tool for conceptualizing social problems, only by examining that wider context can the part played by the Amazon be fully understood.

For the present study, a myth is defined as a story that explains something, for example, life after death or the red of the rose. It is a form of explanation which differs from other types, such as the scientific or philosophical, in several ways. Since it is a story, a myth has a dramatic sequence, a plot, which is composed or extrapolated from everyday realia. Its language, drawn from many areas of society, is free from abstractions and charged with multiple meanings and symbolic values. Mythic explanations are not primarily intended to satisfy intellectual curiosity, nor are they creations solely of the inquiring mind. Myths tend to deal with sources of conflict and tension in the social order and human condition. Their function is to elicit responses to their explanations in the minds and emotions of their receptors in order to obfuscate, circumvent, or mediate those conflicts and tensions. Since resolution is impossible by the principles of reason, a myth manipulates its explanatory techniques in ways that contradict systematic thought. That is not to say that a myth is irrational or illogical in its own terms but that it is other-directed. Its purpose is the diminution of anxiety and resolution of conflict, not truth.

This study inquires into the dynamics of the male/female polarity and the values associated with it throughout Athenian life. Lack of evidence prohibits an investigation into the psychology of personal relationships beyond the social level. How the myth functioned among the individuals who were conditioned by the values assigned to the male/female polarity is unknowable; therefore, we cannot be satisfied with a psychological interpretation. The myth's meaning must be sought in its presentation of a solution to a nagging and perpetual problem that derived from the institutions and norms dictating people's lives. Such a socially and textually oriented interpretation is free of dependency upon outside authority—for example, a Freud or Jung—and imparts to the myth a role in Athenian life that is vital, pervasive, and consonant with Plato's hostility in the *Republic* to the myths of the poets.

The Amazon myth and others included in this study were created by a mythmaking process that drew its plausibility and strength from the data of human physiology. It is given that women's bodies are more devoted to the reproduction of the species than those of men, and that women are engaged in activities having to do with reproduction—whether pregnancy, nursing, or menstruation—most of their adult lives. One impetus to Greek mythmaking founded on these data is a sexual polarization in which the male pole stands for culture and the female pole for nature. Whatever is valued in any area of human concern is defined as culture and thus male, superior, and normal—that is, "the order of things." Nature denotes whatever is not valued by men, and, being judged inferior, abnormal, chaotic, is identified with men's opposite, women. In this mode of mythmaking each pole is absolute and as different from the other as night from a day without twilight.

Persuasive as the sexual polarity is for categorizing phenomena and defining male culture, it is simplistic. Women cannot be identified completely with nature without ignoring their obvious similarities to men. They resemble men and participate in their society more fully than any other being. From this viewpoint the data of their condition support a second mythmaking impetus: the mediation of the polarity of male/female by a third category, which may be called the feminine. The feminine denotes those aspects of the female pole which are similar to the male pole and therefore valued by men. This impetus organizes phenomena according to the scheme male/feminine/female. It gains support in life from the fact that in Greek society women, while bearing children and performing a function of nature, also acculturated the infants through early training, language, etc.; moreover, traditionally, women did the cooking, converting the raw grain of nature into the bread of culture. Although they are the vehicle of society's perpetuation through the children they bear, women are outsiders who import into society the savagery of nature. In mythmaking the female becomes a source of chaos, and the feminine, a means of restoring order. Clytemnestra (female) kills Agamemnon (male), while Electra (feminine) aids the male Orestes.

The following construct of Woman emerges from mythmaking on women's physiological and social condition. Woman is divided into positive and negative elements on a physical and a mental plane. The positive elements, here called the feminine, are defined as her fertility in producing a son and heir and her protection of her husband's household. The latter, the positive mental element, may be seen in Penelope's prolonging of the suitors' wooing through the trick of weaving the shroud until Odysseus returns to slay them. Physicality cast negatively becomes seductive, self-gratifying sexuality, while the negative mental element is characterized as boldness and daring. The negative side of the construct Woman, the female pole, represents in fact no more than the capacity of women to act on their own for their own pleasure and purposes. That potential, defined by Greek polar thinking as destructive to men, is contained by patriarchal marriage; in other words, the bestiality of women's condition is civilized by marriage, which thus becomes in the mythmaking a structure of male order.[2]

Marriage is violated in the myths by both sexes, but with very different consequences. Violations by men, though harmful to women, do not *in themselves* cause the collapse of order. But their actions prompt women in the myths to act, and when that happens, the female is released and marriage is undone as a structure of order. There ensues the downfall of the household, and, if the man is a king or leader, his city plummets into chaos. In Sophocles' *Women of Trachis*, for instance, Heracles intends to replace his wife, Deianira, with a younger woman. Had Deianira not transgressed her place in marriage by trying to hold onto her husband, Heracles' house would have continued, and Deianira alone would have suffered. But she sends to Heracles a poisoned cloak as a love charm, and when he puts it on, his flesh is eaten away by the poison. A woman acting outside marriage and the house—even though she is trying to save both—causes society's loss of a peerless champion, the destruction of his house, and the orphaning of his children.

To explore the problems of women and marriage as they are revealed in the Amazon myth, I have turned to Aeschylus's *Oresteia* for guidance. My reasons are two. The first is that marriage is for Aeschylus a fundamental structure of male order.[3] When Clytemnestra first steps outside it by killing her husband, chaos spreads from the house to the state and cosmos. The second reason derives from the use of myths on the tragic stage. At Athens a play was not an individual effort by a playwright and a company of actors and producers. A tragedy was, first of all, part of a public religious festival conducted by the *polis;* at the same time, it was a social phenomenon in which many people participated first as citizens and then as singers and actors. Through tragedy the city put itself on display, becoming a vehicle for its own propaganda while calling into question its cherished beliefs, unnamed prejudices, and secret anxieties.[4] Tragedy exposed those in the theater to the arbitrariness of the definitions that defended them from the unknown, from the limitlessness that terrified the Greeks. It put on stage people who were faced with deciding what to do in a given situation, but it showed them acting in accepted ways and failing to effect a solution. Tragedy thus disassembles mythic prescriptions and explanations. In the *Oresteia* Aeschylus comes particularly close to the sources of power and upheaval that lie concealed in Athenian mythmaking about Woman as problem. By destroying and re-erecting male order on earth, Aeschylus lays bare the problematics that created the Amazon figure.

Chapter One of the present study traces the history of the Amazon myth at Athens. It follows the myth's use in politics by aristocratic families and its gradual nationalization through the killing of Amazons by individual heroes and their ultimate defeat by all Athenians. There emerges a view of how the myth was developed in the media of vase and mural painting, sculpture, mythography, and funeral oratory by men of means and power in pursuit of their own purposes.

The central question of Chapter Two is the historicity of Amazons in view of the evidence for ancient matriarchies. Such matriarchies are founded on evidence that consists of reversals of patriarchal customs and values. The chapter treats the Cecrops myth of the founding of marriage, Plato's attempt to escape marriage, and Aeschylus's creation of Clytemnestra's matriarchy from the repudiation of marriage.

Chapter Three establishes that the customs of the Amazons are imagined in the myths to be the reverse of those of the patriarchy. Athenian men controlled the outside sphere of war and politics. Amazons fight, hunt, and go campaigning. All other reversals follow from this.

In Chapter Four the Amazons are studied in the light of the rites of transition which every youth had to undergo to become a full member of society. Amazons are figments of the transitional boy and girl who have left social infancy but have not yet been integrated into adulthood. They are one permutation of the female outside marriage—armed, sexual, and dominant.

Chapter Five deals with what it means to kill an Amazon. The Amazon's death is the death of the androgyne. Like Clytemnestra, the Amazon has violently taken male prerogatives of leadership and strength for herself, yet manifests the female aspects of motherhood and religion. The chapter also examines what Aeschylus tells us about the meaning of Clytemnestra's death as a gorgon and as a "daring woman." Both figures symbolize the disintegration of male order into chaos embodied as the woman of independent sexuality and will. They must be killed before order can be restored.

The Amazon belongs to a social dialogue concerning the marriage system. The myth portrays one version of the consequences of the daughter's refusal to leave her mother upon her father's request that she be married. A complete understanding of the myth's meaning, however, can be gained only by placing it within the context of Athenian mythmaking concerning marriage. The *summum bonum* of that discourse is the escape from birth from woman—that is, the attainment of birth from something other than the womb and so something free of the problem of women. In Chapter Six a reading of the trial scene in the final play of the *Oresteia* demonstrates that Aeschylus used the judicial machinery of Orestes' trial as an apparatus to escape birth from women and so the exchange of women in marriage. This examination, then, leads to an understanding of the part played by the Amazon myth in Athenian mythmaking.

AMAZONS: *A Study in Athenian Mythmaking*

·CHAPTER 1·

Amazons and Mythopoiesis

THE GREEKS considered their myths, the tales of gods and heroes, to be a source of instruction. Myths provided precedents  and examples that guided choice by offering actions with known outcomes for imitation or avoidance. Greeks appealed to myths for aid in understanding their lives, for arguments to be used in the art of persuasion, and for rationalizations with which to justify every facet of their lives. For most of them the existence of the myth itself was enough to guarantee the historicity of its events and characters. Arrian, a historian of Alexander, gives a typical response to doubts over the truth of myths. While denying that Amazons were alive in Alexander's day, Arrian refuses to discredit their existence altogether, because of the testimony of "so many illustrious authorities."[1] For the politician seeking a symbol or an orator an illustration, for the poet and painter grateful for a fresh theme or the party-goer in search of a vase for a symposium, what mattered was not truth but the meaning of the Amazons for the individual. This chapter begins the quest for that meaning by following the Amazons' mythopoiesis, "the making of the myth," as it was carried on by men in pursuit of their own aims and goals.

HERACLES' NINTH LABOR

Amazons enter Attic history after 575 B.C. as Heracles' opponents in paintings on black-figure vases. They appear suddenly, in force, and without apparent antecedents.[2] The scene is most likely Heracles' Ninth Labor, the expedition for the Amazon queen's girdle, since no other Amazon adventure is told for him, and one vase represents the fighting as taking place before the Amazons' city of Themiscyra.[3] Nevertheless, the girdle is nowhere depicted, and Heracles' Amazon is usually Andromache, not the Hippolyte of literary tradition. The earliest written version of the myth is given by Euripides in the *Heracles* (c. 417 B.C.):

> He gathered no mean throng of friends from Greece and
> came through the surge of Lake Axine to the mounted host
> of the Amazons to get the gold-decked garment of the dress of
> Ares' daughter, a deadly hunting for a girdle. Greece received
> the famous booty of the foreign maid and keeps it in My-
> cenae.[4]

The Labor is always cast as an expedition of many heroes. Among them, without exception, is Telamon; the Argonauts and Achilles' father, Peleus, were added later. The allusion to Mycenae recalls its king, Eurystheus, and the usual form of the myth, that Heracles was sent by him to fetch the girdle for his daughter.[5] Except for Heracles' companions, however, none of this is discernible from the vase.

The major motifs of the earliest paintings are reproduced on a vase destined for export to Etruria.[6] The Greeks are moving against the Amazons from the left, and combat occurs in pairs. Andromache, knees bent, gives way before Heracles, who is distinguished by his lionskin. He steps on her leg and holds her crest to firm his thrust. Behind him Iphito is victorious over a nameless Greek whose appeal for mercy goes unheeded. Behind Andromache, Telamon kills Glauce. The Amazons are dressed in Greek armor and carry Greek weapons, and their femininity is not stressed.

The Amazons' sudden appearance on black-figure vases may have a political explanation. Pisistratus, the tyrant of Athens from 545 to 527 B.C., sought to identify himself with Heracles as the protégé of the city's goddess, Athena. The evidence is circumstantial, but Pisistratus's return from his second exile (546 B.C.) in a chariot driven by a tall woman dressed as Athena might have been intended to strike a parallel with Athena's introduction of Heracles into Olympus.[7]

By 550 B.C. the formula of paired combatants had broken down, and Heracles' companions were shown assisting him without opponents of their own. Toward the end of the century the scene of Heracles and a single Amazon became popular. About this time, however, several developments brought about a decline in Heraclean Amazonomachies. Artists had exhausted the potential of the black-figure technique. A new method—designated "red-figure" because figures were left clay-red, while background and details were painted—permitted greater freedom of expression and realism. The preoccupation with scenes depicting Heracles in combat with monsters flagged, coinciding with concern for a new, more civilized slayer of Amazons, Theseus.[8]

THESEUS'S RAPE OF AN AMAZON

Theseus had neither Heracles' fame nor his cults in Attica. Not Athenian by birth, he came from Troizen, on the Saronic Gulf, and was the local hero of Marathon and Aphidna in north Attica. His Cretan adventure with the slaying of the Minotaur and the rape of Ariadne reached back to the earliest stratum of Greek mythology, but outside Attica he was little known. An indication of his obscurity is Homer's assignment of the leadership of the Athenian contingent to the Trojan War to Menestheus.[9] But Theseus was destined for greatness at Athens for no other reason than the absence of a rival there. After the expulsion of Pisistratus's son Hippias and the end of the tyranny in 510 B.C., he was adopted by Cleisthenes and his family, the Alcmaeonidae, who were seeking political power by carrying through the enfranchisement of new citizens and by reorganizing the voting system (reforms that were considered democratic). It is likely that they were responsible for casting Theseus as the founder of Athenian democracy, the king who abdicated for his people.[10]

Myths of Theseus were invented and disseminated during the later decades of the sixth century B.C. by singers of epic poems. The epic magnified a city's or a family's traditions—or their most recent conceits—and conferred upon them the legitimacy of age. Poets were always ready to please their audience with a new episode on the local hero, especially one so favored by those in power as Theseus. Many new exploits were sung at this time. Often, as in the Amazon escapade, they were modeled on a deed of Heracles, and in time Theseus came to be dubbed "this other Heracles." By the close of the century a repertoire of incidents had been built up, allowing for the formation of the Theseus myth in a longer poem, the *Theseis*.[11] Evidence for the *Theseis* is scanty, and the following reconstruction is at best plausible.

Theseus goes to Themiscyra with his friend Pirithous and the charioteer Phorbas. He rapes an Amazon and escapes, taking her home to Athens. The Amazons retaliate by invading Attica and laying siege to the Acropolis at Athens. In the month of Boedromion (September) they are driven back in decisive defeat, and a treaty is concluded through the intercession of Theseus's Amazon. Later, like Jason with Medea, Theseus, although he had a son by her, deserts his Amazon for a Greek wife, Phaedra. In revenge the Amazon breaks in on the wedding feast, but is killed by Heracles, who is among the guests.[12]

Another version of Theseus's adventure with the Amazons was current about the same time as the *Theseis*. As early as about 510 B.C. a scene on the Athenian treasury at Delphi made Theseus a part of Heracles' expedition for Hippolyte's girdle, a compromise version used when Heracles' hold on the Amazon was too strong to be undermined by a local upstart.[13] The pro-Thesean poets, however, would not have diminished their hero's glory by subordinating him to another. They surely told the adventure as Theseus's own.

No precedent was needed for the rape; Theseus was notorious for raping Helen and Ariadne in his older myths, as well as the daughters of Cercyon and Sinis in the myths invented by the epic poets.[14] Pirithous was probably included among his followers because he was with Theseus in the rape of Helen. A charioteer was required because the myth was patterned upon Athenian marriage rituals.

In antiquity there was uncertainty over the Amazon's name, a sign of the myth's youth; truly ancient myths have a fixed nomenclature. Vase paintings of the myth give *Antiope,* and this was the name common in the fifth century B.C. *Hippolyte* prevailed in the fourth century; *Melanippe* and *Glauce* also appear.[15]

The myth of the rape was invented, it is generally agreed, to explain the invasion. My assumption that the *Theseis* told of a final battle leading to a truce is based upon the account of the historian of Attica, Cleidemus, which Plutarch quoted in his *Theseus.*[16] Since Cleidemus was writing in the fourth century B.C., and nowhere is any connection with the *Theseis* established for him, the assumption concerning the truce must be defended. The relevant part of Plutarch's narrative reads as follows: "an agreement was reached through the intercession of Hippolyte in the fourth month. Cleidemus gives that name, not Antiope, to the Amazon who married Theseus."

The myth of the rape appeared on the Temple of Apollo Daphnephorus in Eretria about 510 B.C. and on vases, all dating before the Persian wars (490, 480/79 B.C.). It disappeared after the wars, when invading Persians from the East were equated with Amazons. In postwar myths the Amazon is killed fighting with Theseus or against him, and the Amazons themselves are annihilated. In speaking of an agreement and the Amazon surviving the war, Cleidemus has either devised a new conclusion or, though writing late, returned to an earlier form of the myth. The latter is more likely since there was no reason after the Persian wars to have an Amazon fighting for the Greeks. Annihilation, moreover, had long before Cleidemus's time become critical to the exploitation of the Amazon myth in Athenian political propaganda. The fact of an Amazon fighting on the Greek side not only mitigated the intensity of the conflict between Greeks and Persian-Amazons; it undermined the Athenians' stance in the fifth and fourth centuries as the defenders of all Greece against foreign invaders, since the presence of an Amazon in their ranks alluded to the rape and admitted responsibility for the war. Cleidemus had modified Theseus's Cretan adventure in favor of Athens, so he did not adopt this version out of lack of patriotism.[17] More likely he was acting for reasons of historical accuracy. He knew of an older ending which predated the wars—namely, that of the *Theseis*. The name he gave to the Amazon supports this conclusion; Hippolyte was a name available to those who, like the *Theseis*'s poets, did not enroll Theseus in Heracles' expedition.

There is no doubt how the Amazon died in the *Theseis;* Plutarch quotes it with disapproval.

> The uprising that the poet of the *Theseis* has recorded seems clearly a myth and a fiction. Antiope (the poet says) attacked Theseus at his wedding with Phaedra, and Heracles slew her and the other Amazons aiding her.[18]

The myth appears to be a doublet of Theseus's slaying of Centaurs who broke up Pirithous's wedding feast by lusting for the bride, Hippodamia.[19] In later mythology Phaedra is Theseus's wife, who bears him his citizen-sons, Acamas and Demophon, while the Amazon is a concubine and mother of Hippolytus. After the Amazon's death, Phaedra falls in love with Hippolytus, who is chaste and repelled by her advances. Disgraced, Phaedra commits suicide. Since the attempted seduction is Phaedra's mythic *raison d'être*, her presence suggests that the *Theseis* included the birth of a son by the Amazon. Whether his name was always Hippolytus is doubtful; Pindar gives it as Demophon. Since that is the name of the citizen-son, it may be that the Amazon was Theseus's lawful wife in the *Theseis*.[20]

The first indication of the myth of the rape in political parlance comes at a time of upheaval. In 510 B.C. the Alcmaeonidae and several other noble families succeeded, with the help of Spartans, in driving out Hippias and ending the Pisistratid tyranny. Within a few years the Athenian treasury, with its metopes of Theseus's Amazon exploit with Heracles, and the pediment of the Eretrian temple of Apollo with its depiction of the rape, were built.[21] Both point to the Alcmaeonidae for their inspiration. During the period of their exile the Alcmaeonidae had resided at Delphi, where their liberality in rebuilding the god's temple won for them much influence over the oracle. Herodotus openly states—and his sources were Alcmaeonid—that they bribed the priestess of Apollo to declare to all Spartans that it was their duty to free Athens.[22] A treasury glorifying the Athenian hero, suitably subdued for the Panhellenic shrine, can have no other provenance. But the interest of the Alcmaeonidae in Theseus was greater than that expressed for the city's hero: he was their hero too.

After the restoration of the aristocracy, factional struggles resumed, but tyranny had weakened the aristocrats' hereditary hold on the people while strengthening their sense of personal worth. When Cleisthenes, most prominent of the Alcmaeonidae, bid for supremacy by introducing democratic reforms meant to widen participation in government, the other nobles appealed to Sparta for aid. In 507 B.C. the Spartans invaded Attica, the Boeotians attacked from the northwest, and the Chalcidians, age-old rivals of the Eretians in Euboea, attacked from the northeast. The Spartan army advanced as far as Eleusis, where it broke apart in disputes over its purpose. The main threat having melted away before him, Cleisthenes turned the Athenians against the Chalcidians. Herodotus tells us what ensued:

> The Boeotians were coming to the Euripus strait to aid the
> Chalcidians. The Athenians, seeing these reinforcements, decided to attack the Boeotians before the Chalcidians. They
> engaged them and won decisively, killing very many and
> taking seven hundred captive. On the same day they crossed

over into Euboea and engaged the Chalcidians. Defeating them, they left behind four thousand citizen-settlers in the territory belonging to the noble horsemen.[23]

The oligarchs of Eretria had cooperated with aristocrats at Athens in the past and most likely were responsible for transporting the Athenian troops across the strait into Euboea. After the humbling of Chalcis, Eretria's influence in the area surged briefly, then it was extinguished in 490 B.C. when the Persians plundered and burned the city and sold the Eretrians into slavery as punishment for their part in the Ionian Revolt (see below).[24] One of the temples destroyed, whose west pediment perhaps commemorated a wondrous day in 507 B.C., belonged to Apollo Daphnephorus. But the association of the myth of the rape with the Alcmaeonidae may be drawn more tightly.

Vase painters at Athens, like artists everywhere, were always looking for new material. Soon after the west pediment was in place at the Temple of Apollo Daphnephorus, vases imitating it began to appear. One vase, a belly amphora by the potter and painter Myson, is especially revealing.[25] It shows Theseus and Pirithous in full stride to the left. Theseus carries Antiope, his eyes on her, while she appeals with outstretched arms to unseen friends. Pirithous follows, his head turned back on guard. Antiope is dressed in oriental trousers and bears an ax, bow, and quiver. On the other side of the amphora, a man called Euthymus ("he of good spirits") is lighting a pyre. On top sits Croesus, king of Lydia, with a laurel wreath on his head. He is pouring a libation. The scene refers to Croesus's death after his defeat at the hands of the Persian Cyrus (c. 545 B.C.). Later tradition had it that Croesus was saved by Apollo in gratitude for his many dedications of gold and silver to Apollo's oracle at Delphi.[26]

T. B. L. Webster has suggested that the name *Euthymus* and Croesus's festive garb denote Apollo's rescue. The laurel of his wreath is an obvious allusion to the god's sacred tree. The depiction of Theseus's new exploit on a vase with Croesus, himself connected with Apollo and the source of the Alcmaeonid fortune, points to the Alcmaeonidae as the source of the painting.[27] Perhaps an Alcmaeonid commissioned Myson for the amphora.

One family of aristocrats adopted the Amazon as its logotype, but in this form the myth was short-lived. The preeminence of the Alcmaeonidae passed away with Cleisthenes. Rape, however heroic when practiced on foreigners, remained, in Herodotus's words, "the act of a rascal." It ill-befitted the national champion and humane king, the fifth-century Theseus. After the Persian wars, the Amazon myth took another direction. The myth of the rape entered written tradition when about 475 B.C. the mythographer Pherecydes wrote it down in his handbook.[28]

THESEUS'S DEFENSE OF ATHENS

In 499 B.C. the Greeks in Ionia revolted against Persia; four years later they were crushed and their leading city of Miletus was destroyed. Eretria and Athens sent ships to aid the revolt and joined in the burning of Sardes, capital of Lydia. The Persian king, Darius, moved to engulf the mainland Greeks, the Athenians in particular. His quest for vengeance failed in 490 B.C. on the plain of Marathon before a small force of Athenians and Plataeans. Ten years later Darius's son, Xerxes, invaded the West by land and sea. The war lasted two years (480–79) and ended with the expulsion of the foreigners from Greece. In 478 B.C. Athens assumed the leadership of the Delian League, an alliance of Hellespontine, Ionian, and island states against the Persians in the eastern Aegean. It was the first step toward the splendor and suffering of imperial Athens.[29]

The development of the Amazon myth resumes in an atmosphere of intense antipathy toward Persians and other foreigners, whom the Greeks called *barbaroi* from the sound of their language, the "bar-bar" of twittering birds. Victory had awakened the Athenians, stirring in them new confidence and a drive for accomplishments. Also at this time they became aware of the paucity of their heroic past and the need to expand upon it in order to substantiate their pretensions abroad.

On the Theseum

The mood of postwar Athens was first exploited by Cimon, the leading member of the aristocratic Philaedae and son of Miltiades, hero of Marathon. Cimon was vigorously implementing the Delian League's aggression toward Persia. In a move combining religious piety with mythic propaganda and naked imperialism, the Athenians obtained a Delphic oracle charging them with returning Theseus's bones to a place of honor in Athens. Tradition said that Theseus had been treacherously murdered and was buried on the island of Scyros. In 476/75 B.C. a naval force under Cimon captured Scyros, sold its non-Greek inhabitants into slavery, and colonized it with Athenians. Bones were found and installed in Theseus's sanctuary.[30]

The Theseum was located in the middle of Athens, southwest of the agora. It appears to have consisted of a sizable precinct and at least one building, which housed the hero's tomb and had walls large enough for paintings. The foremost muralists, Micon and Polygnotus, painted scenes from Theseus's life: the recovery of Minos's ring from the bottom of the sea, the fighting with the Lapiths against the Centaurs at Pirithous's wedding feast, an Amazonomachy, and, probably, the rescue from Hades after the failure to abduct Persephone. The Amazonomachy, most likely done by Polygnotus, was the first to depict the battle for the Acropolis.[31]

The Theseum was a harbinger of Athens' imperialism since Scyros was seized to benefit its naval operations in the Aegean. Even so, the ambience surrounding the enshrining of the bones evoked memories of the sixth century in that it continued the absorption of aristocratic cults by the state, a practice Pisistratus had begun. The Theseia, or Festival of Theseus, was made part of the religious calendar for the eighth day of the month of Pyanepsion (late October), the day after the Oschophoria, a festival already linked with Theseus. The former owners of the rites of Theseus, the aristocratic Phytaedae, were reduced to caretakers. At this time a sacrifice to the Amazons was inaugurated, probably by usurping an existing rite. Also taken over in Theseus's name was a holy area near his shrine, the Horcomosium, the name of which was interpreted as denoting the place where Theseus and the Amazons swore the oath (*horkos*) that ended the war.[32]

Another evocation of the sixth century was the political purpose the murals served. Cimon intended them to strike a parallel between Theseus's achievements and his own. Like Cimon, Theseus defeated a sea power (Minos) and overcame foes who were savage (Centaurs) and foreign/Eastern (Amazons). Mythically, the murals followed the *Theseis*'s technique of depicting Theseus on the pattern of Heracles. The latter fought Centaurs and Amazons and was received into Olympus by his father, Zeus; Theseus fought the same enemies and was received into his father Poseidon's palace when he went to retrieve Minos's ring. Heracles probably appeared in one painting since it was he who liberated Theseus from the underworld. Evidence from vase paintings that reproduce the Amazonomachies of the Theseum and Stoa Poikile (see below) suggests that Polygnotus followed the *Theseis* in putting an Amazon on Theseus's side. In 476 B.C., then, the invasion myth was above all a feat in the life of the Athenian national hero. Everything was subordinated to him. By the time Cimon returned to the myth for the Stoa Poikile, which was finished about 460 B.C., that had changed.

On the Stoa Poikile

Soon after the Athenians' triumph over the Persians at Eurymedon in 469 B.C., Cimon probably began plans for a porch on the north side of the agora. It was built by Pisianax, an Alcmaeonid and relative of Cimon's by marriage. The porch was an open row of columns, enclosed at the ends by a short wall and paralleled by another. Pisianax called it the Stoa Pisianactea, but it was soon dubbed the Stoa Poikile, or Painted Porch, after the paintings it sheltered. The paintings were done on boards affixed to the walls and showed Athenians confronting Lacedaemonians at Oine, Amazons before the Acropolis, Persians and Greeks at Marathon, and the capture of Troy.[33] The Stoa was a popular spot in the life of the city, and its paintings were famous in antiquity. It ranks with the Theseum as a disseminator of the Amazon myth.

Nothing is known directly about the composition of the Stoa's Amazonomachy except that the artist was Micon and that he painted Amazons mounted and with wicker shields.[34] Vases dating after 470 B.C. and confined mostly to the school of the Niobid Painter provide clues, but there is no way to distinguish the influence of the Stoa from that of the Theseum. The most striking feature of these vases is the depiction of combatants on several levels. Landscape is indicated by plants and trees. The murals may have represented the battle as being waged on level ground near the hill of the Acropolis. They may also have shown two Greeks, one in armor and the other nude, striding to the right and armed with spears. Amazons were dressed in checkered trousers and boots and, in some instances, diaphanous clothing, a technique introduced by Polygnotus.[35]

Although no distinction between the scenes of the Stoa and those of the Theseum may be drawn from the motifs of the vases, John P. Barron has suggested a means of determining which version of the myth each followed.[36] From a telltale mistake in anatomy—the division of the male abdomen into four sections instead of the normal three—he has concluded that the Centauromachy on the neck of the calyxcrater in New York (the work of the Painter of the Woolly Satyrs) imitated the same scene on the Theseum mural. It therefore seems likely that the crater's major scene, an Amazonomachy, also was copied from the Theseum. The Amazonomachy on the New York crater, Barron contends, is closely connected in spirit and motifs with one done on a crater by the Painter of the Berlin Hydria. The latter vase shows an Amazon fighting on the side of the Greeks. If Barron is correct in joining these two scenes, and if they both do go back to one original, then the Amazon, who must be Theseus's wife, was fighting on his side in the Theseum mural. Other vases showing Theseus and the Amazon opposed to each other must reproduce the Stoa version. Cimon followed the myth of the attack on Athens told in the *Theseis,* a suggestion that is likely on its own merits, since a friendly

Amazon had no place in the equation of Amazons and Persians that was made in funeral oratory after the Theseum's magnification in 475 B.C.

In Funeral Oratory

The Athenians were unique among Greeks for burying the dead from the previous summer's military campaigning in a common grave at home in the public cemetery in the suburb of Ceramicus.[37] A board chosen by lot selected a pillar of the community to pronounce a eulogy over them. The ceremony must have been a common occurrence during the militant years after the Persian wars. The speeches themselves lauded Athens and its past and were quickly rendered formulaic by the expectations of the audience and the oratorical modesty of those who delivered them. They followed a pattern of praise of the dead, lament, and consolation.[38] The first speeches dealt with the ancestors of the dead, their accomplishments, and the feats of their progeny. Eulogizers dwelled upon the mythic past, citing a complex of deeds which testified to the primacy of Athenians among the Greeks and to their self-sacrifice in maintaining Greek freedom and customs. The defeat of the Amazons was praised as the rescue of all Greeks from slavery at the hands of foreign conquerors. Theseus and the rape of the Amazon were forgotten, and the exploit was turned into one belonging to all Athenians. A speech attributed by Herodotus to the Athenians on the fields of Plataea illustrates how such rhetoric treated the Amazon myth. The Athenians are pleading their case for having leadership of the left wing of the Greek army:

> It is incumbent upon us to show you the origin of our national heritage, by which we claim on past bravery to be first before the Arcadians. The sons of Heracles, whose leader the Tegeans say they killed at the isthmus, we alone received after they were driven out by all Greeks to whom they came in flight from enslavement under the Myceneans. We humbled Eurystheus's pride, defeating in battle those who controlled the Peloponnesus at that time. We made an expedition against

the Cadmeans of Thebes, where we buried the bodies of those Argives who attacked the city with Polynices and, perishing there, were left unburied. We have the successful exploit against the Amazons from the Thermodon River who once invaded Attica. In the Trojan War we were inferior to none. . . . Let this suffice for past exploits. If we had performed no other success—even though ours are as numerous as yours and others of the Greeks—from that one in Marathon we would be worthy of having this honor and others besides. We alone of the Greeks, fighting the Persian by ourselves and taking in hand a great task, prevailed and conquered forty-six nations.[39]

To understand the significance of the change in the myth, it is necessary to consider the effects upon the Athenians of their expansionism in the Aegean. The Delian League began as an alliance against Persia but turned into an empire for Athens. Several factors contributed to this erosion of allies into subjects. Athens alone formulated policy and benefited from success, since individual states were allied with it, not with each other. Though free to contribute money or ships, most states preferred money and ended by funding a fleet for Athens. When Naxos revolted (468 B.C.?) and was forced back into membership, Athens betrayed itself as an empire city. All pretense was dropped after the league's treasury was transferred from Delos to Athens about 454. The result was a growing fear and hatred of the Athenians (the eventual cause of the Peloponnesian War) and the Athenians' own isolation from the rest of the Hellenic world.[40]

According to Kenneth R. Walters,

[T]hese speeches fulfilled an important, indeed vital, social function for the Athenians. However hackneyed its themes may seem, the funeral oration was a true *vox populi*: it promulgated a message that was hardly the personal expression of the orators, but rather the collective voice of the Athenian polity. In sum, the orations were designed not to inform or to innovate, but to articulate in ritual fashion shared

community ideals, values, and attitudes. In particular, they
expressed and sought to resolve troubling inconsistencies
and contradictions that were the legacy of Athenian culture
and history.[41]

Nevertheless, unremitting imperialism from the founding of the
Delian League until final defeat and loss of empire in 404 B.C. en-
gendered among the Athenians a contradiction between their
claim to be defenders of Greek freedom and their actual suppression of it. Funeral oratory distorted and falsified mythical and historical events; it created a myth, a reality of words, which explained
aggression as assistance and altruism and which transformed isolation from that of a tyrannical city into the desertion of Athenians
by other Greeks, a desertion which left them the solitary defenders
of the common cause.[42] Both distortions are found in Herodotus's
speech. The battle of Marathon was won, not by the Athenians
alone, but with the aid of Plataeans, for whose service—everyone
knew—blessings from the gods were evoked during the Panathenaea and four other festivals. Only in funeral oratory was violence
required to release those killed with Polynices for burial; elsewhere, the Thebans returned the dead peacefully and without
coercion.[43] These facts were well known but irrelevant in the face
of the community's need for a message proclaiming the righteousness of its violence. The changes made in the Amazon myth follow
from that purpose. The rape had to be forgotten because it attributed responsibility for the invasion to Theseus and Athens,
while a peaceful settlement arranged by Theseus's Amazon took
away the excuse for the exercise of righteous violence, the justification of which was the myth's purpose in funeral oratory.

Once the rape was suppressed, another reason for the invasion
had to be supplied. Funeral orators imputed to the Amazons their
own motivations; now they invaded Attica in order to spread
their empire over Greeks. The following quotation is from the
Panegyricus (380 B.C.) of the Athenian orator Isocrates. Though
not a funeral oration, it includes the traditional catalog of mythic
exploits:

When Greece was still humble, the Thracians invaded the land with Eumolpus, son of Poseidon, and the Scythians with the Amazons, daughters of Ares. They did not come at one time but when each would extend its dominion over Greece. Though they hated the whole Greek race, they brought charges against us, thinking that in this way they would take risks against one city and gain mastery over all. They did not succeed. Engaging our ancestors alone, they were destroyed just as if they had waged war against all mankind. The magnitude of their disasters is clear, for otherwise reports concerning them would not have survived for so long. Of the Amazons it is said that not one of those who came returned, and those left behind were driven from their empire on account of the catastrophe here.[44]

Isocrates reproduces the theme of solitary Athens as savior of Greece. His Amazons are not the avengers of the *Theseis* but are empire builders like the Athenians. This view, not original with Isocrates, is found as early as 458 B.C. in Aeschylus's *Eumenides*. Aeschylus derived the name of the Areopagus (hill of Ares) at Athens from the Amazons who sacrificed there to Ares when they came "with an army in spite toward Theseus and built towers against this new, lofty-towered city."[45] The change from invading female avengers to female imperialists provides an insight into Athenian mythmaking. Avengers are overcome and expelled in much the same way as invading Persians; thus Demosthenes boasts in his funeral oration that they were driven beyond the Phasis River—that is, beyond the eastern border of the West.[46] But Amazon imperialists oppose Athenian imperialists as women oppose men. Should the Amazons be victorious, women would rule over men as men ruled in everyday life over women. That specter of the imagination had to be eliminated through total annihilation. Lysias, in a funeral oration perhaps eulogizing one year's dead during the Corinthian War (395–86 B.C.), carries the mythmaking process further:

Long ago there were Amazons, daughters of Ares, who lived along the Thermodon River. They alone of the peoples around them were armed with iron, and they were the first to ride horses. With them, because of the inexperience of their enemies, the Amazons slew those who fled and outran those who pursued. For their bravery Amazons used to be considered men rather than women for their physical nature. They seemed to surpass men in their spirit instead of falling short of them in appearance. They ruled many lands and enslaved their neighbors. Then, hearing of the great renown of this land, they gathered their most warlike nations and marched against the city. A glorious reputation and high ambitions were their motives. But here they met brave men and came to possess spirits alike to their nature. Gaining a reputation that was the opposite of the one they had, they appeared women because of the dangers rather than from their bodies. For them alone it was impossible to learn from their mistakes and form better plans about the future. Since they did not go home, they could not announce their misfortunes nor the bravery of our ancestors, for they died here and paid the penalty for their folly. They made the memory of the city imperishable because of its bravery and rendered their own country nameless because of their disaster here. Those women who unjustly lusted after another's land justly lost their own.[47]

Lysias draws two oppositions between the Amazons and their neighbors: iron weapons/no iron weapons and horses/no horses. In these oppositions the neighbors represent the reality of Athenian fighting. Athenians fight against men who have the same kind of weapons; Amazons have superior weapons and so gain easy victory. Athenians must stand in a formation and cannot run away, because the safety of all depends upon the cohesiveness of the formation and because of their heavy arms; Amazons flee on swift horses whenever they are endangered. Lysias is inventing details about the Amazons by reversing the manner of Athenian fighting. It is significant that he does not embellish the myth freely but creates polar oppositions to what is the male way of things among the Greeks.

Lysias describes the makeup of the Amazons by the same process of polarization. The male prerogatives of ruling lands, enslaving neighbors, and pursuing a reputation are given to the Amazons. But Lysias does not assign the Amazons' female attributes to the Athenians; the Amazons, while gaining male attributes, retain their female bodies. The result is a sexual hybrid. Amazons are not women in male armor but are androgynes—apparitions composed of male and female elements which confuse the distinctions between the sexes and the values and categories of thought assigned to each. Lysias therefore cannot be satisfied with killing them; he must reduce them through the "dangers" of combat to mere women, single-sexed beings who have female spirits as well as natures.

The bravery displayed by the Athenians is the Homeric *aretē*, a term designating the qualities of the man victorious in war and prosperous in peace. For the Homeric warrior, as for the classical Greek, actions were characterized as *aretē* if they proved his prowess, thereby winning him undying fame. Since life after death was a joyless continuance, a man's reputation had to be secured so that his memory would remain among the living to console him in death. Winning was paramount; losing conferred disgrace and oblivion.[48] This system of values explains Lysias's claim that the Amazons' death rendered the reputation of Athens imperishable while effacing their name from memory.

The references to justice appear straightforward, but the term has a specialized connotation in funeral orations. The Athenians claimed to be born from the earth, and therefore they were just because they had not driven others out of Attica and seized their land.[49] This metaphysical justice of autochthony (birth from the earth itself) was another element in the message of righteous violence. Anxiety over their imperialism was soothed by the belief that men just by virtue of their birth could do no wrong. The defeat of the Amazons—imperialists like themselves, but (not being autochthonous) unjust ones—is asserted as proof the Athenians' "just" birth.

Judging from Lysias's efforts, funeral orations were a formative medium in introducing the Amazon myth into the mainstream of Athenian life. Their complex of mythic precedents appears in part on the Stoa Poikile, and Aeschylus's reliance in the *Oresteia* upon the audience's familiarity with their themes and motifs cannot be unique. The Athenian myth of the Amazons achieved its most significant expression, however, in the religion of the Parthenon.

On the Parthenon

The Parthenon stood on the south side of the Acropolis and presented its west façade to those entering from the Propylaea. The statues of its metopes and pediments, with the exception of the south metopes, have been destroyed or mutilated, many beyond certain identification. The west pediment showed the contest of Athena and Poseidon for the city, while the metopes below it depicted the battle of Amazons and Athenians for the city's Acropolis. Along the north side the metopes portrayed scenes from the sack of Troy; along the south, the battle of Lapiths and Centaurs. In the east pediment, above the entrance to the temple, was displayed the birth of Athena from Zeus's head. The goddess was shown fully grown and armed with a helmet and shield, looking back at her father as she moved to the right. Zeus sat enthroned in the center with the scepter and thunderbolt, lord of the scene. The east metopes depicted the battle of the Olympians and earth-born Giants. Inside the Parthenon's east cella stood Phidias's chryselephantine colossos of Athena Parthenos. The outside of her shield depicted in relief another Amazonomachy; the inner side, in paint, a Gigantomachy.[50]

Athena Polias, Athena of the city, was worshiped on the north side of the Acropolis in the Erechtheum. To that temple, even after the construction of the Parthenon, was directed the procession of all Athenians in the Panathenaea. It was the center for her worship as the city's tutelary deity. The Parthenon, on the other hand, was financed by tribute from the empire and was intended by a single generation of Athenians to be a witness to "the ever-lasting glory" of their accomplishments.[51] Its goddess, although not distinguished from Athena of the Erechtheum by any specific term, belonged to the men of Periclean Athens. "To the Pericleans," observes C. J. Herington, "Athena *is* Athens; the best that Athens stands for. Athena's attributes, victorious prowess in war, intelligence, love of the arts, are precisely the attributes of the Athenian people as Pericles describes them in the Funeral Speech." This Athena was the product of "a certain balance of thought and politics" that ended with the death of Pericles and the loss of empire.[52] In that moment during the fifth century B.C. a generation found its sense of self in its mythic tradition. On the Parthenon the Amazon myth was integrated into an ideology that consciously blended religious conviction with patriotism.

The east façade, the Parthenon's primary side, juxtaposed the birth of Athena and the battle of the Olympians and Giants. The first scene affirms Athena's close relationship with her father, Zeus, and the favor accruing to her and her people from him. In overcoming the Giants, Athena realized the promise of her birth—the triumph of civilization over wanton violence.[53] The same theme was projected by the Centauromachy, where violence is represented as beasts, by the Trojan scene against Asians, and by the Amazonomachy against women. These sculptures convey a consistent message: the Athenians possess a land worthy of divine strife and are a people who have overcome the forces of barbarism under the special protection of their goddess, the delight of her father, Zeus.

Amazons appear twice in the religion of the Parthenon. Their defeat in the west metopes contrasts with Athena's victory in the pediment. One warrior-maiden successfully gives her name to the city, while the annihilation of the others affirms that it is under male control. The second Amazonomachy on Phidias's shield has been lost, but copies indicate that Athenians and Amazons were grouped in counterclockwise order around a gorgon's head. This scene holds the meaning and power of the Amazon in Athenian mythmaking and will be analyzed in Chapter Six.

IN WORDS SUNG AND WRITTEN

Meanwhile the myth was being developed in other media. Sometime before 475 B.C. Pherecydes recorded the myth in his mythological handbook. He named Ares and the nymph Harmonia as the Amazons' parents and followed the *Theseis* in giving Theseus his own expedition to the Thermodon. The myth does not seem to have been the subject of a tragedy or comedy, but Euripides' *Hippolytus* (428 B.C.) is concerned with the Amazons' rejection of marriage through the son of Theseus's Amazon. In the *Suppliant Women* (c. 463 B.C.) Aeschylus calls the Amazons "manless and meat-eating," a reference not to their diet but to their savage state as meat-eaters, as opposed to civilized Greeks, who eat bread.[54]

Toward the end of the fifth century B.C., Hellanicus, an Ionian from Lesbos, published the first history of Attica. His description of the Amazons as "a golden-shielded, silver-axed, female, male-loving, male-infant-killing host" suggests an extensive treatment of the myth. According to Hellanicus the Amazons crossed over into Greece on the frozen Bosphorus and removed their right breasts by cauterization. The first detail he drew most likely from Herodotus, who attributed that means of access to the Scythians; the second, from the Hippocratic treatise *Airs, Waters, Places*.[55]

Hellanicus was a scholar and a foreigner who provided the Athenians with a work of Ionian historiography. It served until the middle of the next century, when the first history written by a citizen, the *Atthis* of Cleidemus, appeared. A succession of histories then ensued, ending with Philochorus's in 261 B.C. Why, after such a long period, was Hellanicus's work replaced by those of citizens? Perhaps, as has been suggested, the composition of the history of all of Greece, the *Hellenica*, popular since Xenophon's continuation of Thucydides' history, went out of fashion, to be replaced by local histories.[56] Perhaps also the threat from Philip of Macedonia to the independence of the city encouraged Athenians to reexamine their past. What seems clear, however, is that these histories were not politically motivated.[57] Philochorus was a scholar of religious rites and customs. Nothing is known about his treatment of the Amazonomachy nor about the renderings by the Atthidographers before him. Cleidemus put his account together from sites around the city, events of the sacred calendar, and earlier tradition. Plutarch followed this account for his *Theseus.*[58]

The Amazon myth was developed by men in charge of the media. They elaborated upon its two primary episodes, Heracles' Ninth Labor and the invasion of Attica, thereby generating a picture of the Amazons and their customs by drawing upon the data of gender roles and values. They emphasized on the conscious level the clash of arms more than the sexual conflict, as Apollo's outcry in the *Eumenides* indicates. If Agamemnon had to be cut down by a woman, Apollo laments, why could it not have been by an Amazon?[59] The Athenians thought about the Amazon first as a warrior and then as a woman. The meaning that emerges at first glance is one of triumph over enemies who have been equated with women.

·CHAPTER 2·

Amazons
and Matriarchy

WERE THERE EVER Amazons? May we dismiss them out of hand? Most Greeks believed that they existed at one time, and

the report of their attack on Athens appears ancient. There is, in fact, no way historically to deny their existence and no way to prove it. The evidence from classical Athens, as we have seen, bears witness to the myth, not to Amazons *qua* Amazons. Archaeologists have thus far not uncovered the remains of an Amazon grave or city, and the Greeks did not find any when they arrived on the Thermodon.

THE QUESTION OF EXISTENCE

It is possible, however, that the myth began with reality. Stories of mounted and armed nomad women could have been brought from the hinterlands of Asia Minor and the Black Sea to the Greeks on the Ionian coast and on to Athens. Herodotus calls the Amazons *Oiorpata,* which means "man-killer" in Scythian.[1] The Scythians were nomads living north of the Black Sea. On the other hand, theories based on men as the myth's source betray a chauvinistic bias (men alone can fight, so *cherchez l'homme*) and are belied by Herodotus's account of the ancestry of the Sauromatians.[2]

The Sauromatians were said to be descended from Scythians and Amazons. The latter, taken in the battle on the Thermodon and put into ships bound for Greece, killed their captors and, as they knew nothing of sailing, were carried to Lake Maiotis in Scythia. At first the Scythians fought them, but when they discovered their sex from the corpses, they sent their youngest men courting. The same power to discriminate between the sexes may be granted the Greeks.

Alexander was supposed to have enjoyed an affair with an Amazon queen in Bactria in 329 B.C.. The story is told in much the same way by three authors, a sign of a common source.[3] Thalestris, eminent for her beauty and prowess, is attracted by Alexander's renown and comes to him. Leaving most of her army behind, she arrives with a guard of three hundred Amazons. She wants "to make child" with him, he consents, and they stay together for thirteen days. Much later, when Lysimachus, an officer under Alexander's command, heard the story, he smiled and asked, "And where was I at the time?"[4]

What are we to make of the incident? Plutarch, who related the anecdote about Lysimachus, discounted it without questioning the existence of Amazons. One episode, probably derived from the daily journal kept by Alexander, may account for the Amazon Thalestris. A Scythian king came to Bactria, according to Arrian, to offer his daughter in marriage.[5] The king of Chorasmia, the country east of the Caspian Sea, also was in Bactria. Greek scuttlebutt arising from the resemblance to their Amazons of a nomad princess who could ride and shoot a bow reached the Chorasmian king. He volunteered to lead Alexander against his neighbors the Amazons, perhaps as an added incentive for an alliance. Amazons were on people's minds in Bactria, and Thalestris was the result.

We are, however, no closer to proving—or disproving—the existence of Amazons. Militant women may be the myth's historical core, but these women lived and fought in societies dominated by men. Amazons controlled the family, the state, and its institutions;

they dominated men in a matriarchy, another matter altogether. If matriarchal societies could be shown to exist, the possibility of an Amazon version would gain credibility.

In 1861 Johann Jacob Bachofen published *Das Mutterrecht* [*The Mother Right*], in which he contended that all cultures had evolved to patriarchy from matriarchy.[6] His thesis, based on intuition and the eschewal of field work, is condemned by contemporary anthropologists. Bachofen gleaned his evidence mainly from myths he equated with history, an unfounded and simplistic assumption. This is particularly the case for the ancient Greeks, who regarded myths as history because they told of universal truths, not the details we deem to be historical facts. Evidence taken by Bachofen to prove matriarchy attests rather to matriliny. In groups governed by matrilineal descent, men, not women, have authority, albeit these men are brothers and uncles rather than husbands and fathers (the pattern in patrilineal descent groups). Thus, the case for matriarchy provides no support for the historicity of Amazons. They remain moot, and, as it stands, there is no profit in rehearsing the theories of their origins, since such theories comment at best upon the origin of the myth, not its meaning for Athenians and ancient Greeks in general. The conclusion of a scholar who happens also to be a woman corroborates my reservations while inclining toward the possibility of an Amazon society:

> Since there is nothing inherently monstrous or impossible about an Amazonian society, it is possible, though of course, not provable, that such a society did exist.
>
> Without making any determination as to the historical veracity of the Amazons, we are on safer ground when we deal with the importance of the Amazons to the Greeks as well as to the modern world as a concept.[7]

We now move to that more fruitful territory of matriarchy the concept, that is, the myth.

GREEK PATRIARCHY

From our first evidence, Homer's epics, the Greek world is patri-archal. In the *Iliad,* Hector rebukes a wife who would advise him on strategy by affirming the classic gender roles of the patriarchy:

> Go into the house and see to your tasks, the loom and the distaff, and bid your handmaidens go about their task. War will concern men, all those born at Troy and me especially.[8]

Herodotus provides a model of the ideal life for man and woman in his report of a supposed conversation between Solon and Croesus. They are discussing who is the happiest of all men. A man's life, as described by Solon, is his city, his health, and his sons, the future of his household; a woman's life is the state religion and her sons. The vignette is all the more revealing for being beside Herodotus's point:

> Tellos lived while his city was flourishing. He had fine brave sons and saw children born to each, and all survived. He prospered as life is with us, and his end proved to be most glorious. A fight broke out between the Athenians and their neighbors from Eleusis. Tellos answered the cry for help and routed the enemy. He died very nobly, and the Athenians buried him at public expense where he fell, and honored him greatly. . . .The Argives Cleobis and Biton had sufficient livelihood, and both were champions in the games. When time for the festival to Hera came, the story goes, they yoked themselves to a cart and conveyed their mother to the temple because the oxen had not yet come in from the fields. Pressed by the hour, they put on the yoke and began drawing the wagon with their mother. They came to the temple after a journey of five miles. . . . The Argive men gathered around and called them blessed for their strength. The Argive women deemed the mother blessed for having such children.[9]

Patriarchy is a form of social organization based on dominance, the dominance of men over women, husband over wife, father over mother and children, older man over younger, and the father-line over the mother-line. As Aristotle pronounces in the *Politics*, "The male is by nature more suited to rule than the female (except where the household has been set up contrary to nature) and the elder and more mature more than the younger and immature."[10] The core of Athenian patriarchy is the household (*oikos*). On it depended the individual and the state, and it, in turn, depended for survival on its economic resources and on marriage to bring in new members. The source of both is the man: breadwinner and defender, husband and father. Through him the children acquire legitimacy and recognition by the state, and the state is supplied with citizens and warriors. Through him alone the woman has social existence; she is under a man's legal mastery and protection all her life.[11] Her sole purpose is to produce children—in particular, male children.

The ideal of marriage has been exquisitely captured by the Achilles Painter on a lekythos dating from about 440 B.C.[12] The scene, a warrior's farewell to his wife, depicts the inside/outside polarity of marriage. The woman is seated and her scarf or headdress, mirror, and jug hang on the wall; the scene is indoors, in the women's chambers. The man stands before her, his departure imminent. His helmet and shield correspond to her accouterments on the wall, the tools of their separate spheres in marriage. Hers are for beauty and allurement; his, for defense. That theme is present in the shield's profile of an eye. Turned toward her, it connotes protection and watchfulness; more often the eye was done in full as an apotropaic device. The couple's sexual relationship is suggested by transparent clothing. Contrasting sharply with this scene is that of the Penthesilea cup by the Berlin Painter.[13] Achilles drives his sword into the Amazon Penthesilea in a sexually violent portrayal of the Amazon dysfunction of marriage. Order between the sexes, which is maintained by the rigidly discrete gender roles of the patriarchy, is confounded when Penthesilea, a woman, challenges Achilles in battle. He reasserts the norm with his sword/phallus.

MATRIARCHY AS MYTH

In classifying the rule of the household and state, polar thinking limited the Greeks to two alternatives: rule by men or rule by women. No middle, or third, course was imaginable; the absence of rule by men presupposed, on the domestic level, the breakdown of marriage, the death of the husband, and the destruction of his household. On the public level, loss of male rule meant the creation of a matriarchy, a situation tantamount to chaos in the state and cosmos. In the Cecrops myth, matriarchy resulted from the absence of marriage; in Plato's *Republic,* from the philosopher's attempt to escape the ills of marriage; and in Aeschylus's *Agamemnon,* from Clytemnestra's repudiation of marriage. In each of these cases marriage was a structure or construct symbolizing order, and matriarchy was a construct made by reversing the gender roles of marriage. Whatever its historical status, in the classical period matriarchy functioned as a tool for thinking, explaining, and validating patriarchal customs, institutions, and values by postulating the absurdities and horrors of its opposite.[14]

Cecrops's Founding of Marriage

The Athenians attributed the establishment of marriage to Cecrops, their first king and ancestral parent. His form was originally that of a serpent, born of the earth, which, by shedding its skin, symbolized immortality in ancient religions. He was the embodiment of the vigor and identity of the Athenian people and was reincarnated in each of his descendants.[15] After the meaning of his serpentine form was forgotten, Cecrops was shown as human above the waist and serpentine below. Although he is ancient, evidence for his founding of marriage is late, coming from a myth told by the Roman scholar Varro in the first century B.C. and from "learnèd" commentary on Cecrops's twin nature. The latter, though wide of the mark, tells us much about Greek views of matriarchy. It is unlikely that Varro and the others invented Cecrops's role in the transition to patriarchal marriage; nevertheless, no evidence for it has survived from the classical period.[16]

Varro recounts the myth of Cecrops to explain how Athens received its name. When Cecrops was king, Varro says, there suddenly appeared on the Acropolis an olive tree and a spring. The king was alarmed and consulted Apollo's oracle at Delphi. Apollo told him that the olive was the sign of Athena and the spring the sign of Poseidon and that it was incumbent on the people to decide which god they preferred to have as their city's namesake and tutelary deity.

> After receiving the oracle, Cecrops convened all the citizens
> of both sexes to take a vote. (It was the custom at that time
> for women to participate in public deliberations.) The
> men voted for Poseidon, and the women for Athena. And as
> one more woman was found than man, Athena won. Po-
> seidon was enraged and devastated Attica with surging waves.
> . . . To placate his wrath, Varro says that the women were
> punished in three ways: they no longer could cast a vote, no
> new-born child would take the mother's name, and no one
> should call the women Athenians.[17]

Women in Cecrops's Athens have access to authority. They take part in public debate and vote on issues, and since legitimacy and descent are reckoned through the mother, they determine the continuity of the family line. Before the fateful decision, men and women presumably split their vote, and the question of which sex had the majority never arose. But the contest between the gods polarizes them, and they vote on sexual lines. The women turn out to have control—that is, a matriarchy. Such effrontery invites Poseidon's ire, and the women lose the suffrage and matriliny. They are isolated from authority in the state and in the family, a situation which their third punishment reflects: they are no longer called Athenians but daughters of Athenians.

Fundamental to patriarchy are the prohibition of women from

public affairs and patriliny, so the principle of reversal is evident in the myth. No pretense is offered to conceal the founding of the patriarchy on male strength: the women vote the wrong way, offend a powerful god, and lose their rights fair and square.[18] Men are not to blame, because it was not their strength but a god's that caused the women's downfall. The myth not only justifies the lowly estate of women in society; through the contest motif it also diffuses tension between the sexes. The contest elevates the conflict from the human plane to the divine. Harmony exists—at women's expense—on earth, where it counts, because responsibility for women's disenfranchisement has been projected to the heavens.

The relevant commentary is as follows:

At Athens Cecrops first yoked one woman to one man. Before then mating was at random and promiscuous. Hence some think that he was considered twin-natured because before him no one knew the father since there were so many.

Marriage was first discovered at Athens by Cecrops. From this Charax says that he is called twin-natured. On account of him men first recognized that they were begotten from two.

Cecrops had the upper parts of a man and the lower parts of a beast, and for this reason he was twin-natured. Or, it was because he discovered many laws for humans and led them from savagery [or bestiality] to tameness [or civilization].[19] Or, it was because men had intercourse with women as it chanced and so the son was not known to the father nor the father to the son. Cecrops laid down laws so that men had intercourse with them openly and were contented with one wife. He also discovered the two natures of the father and the mother.

Cecrops legislated that women, who before mated like beasts, be given in marriage to one man.[20]

Two imperatives of patriarchy underlie the commentary: through marriage men restrict a woman's sexuality to one man and ensure that the son she bears is that man's and no other's. The reverse situation—women in charge of their own bodies—makes it impossible to identify the son with the father, a situation which in Greek polar thinking is deemed sexual abandon and bestiality. The rationale is that marriage acts to contain the sexual passion of women, thereby protecting society and the family from the pollution of bastardy. In the absence of marriage, sexual drives must run wild.

Matriarchy is constructed or imagined in a series of oppositions correlated with Cecrops's twin nature as human and beast.

Human	Beast
men	women
marriage	promiscuity
fatherhood	motherhood
identity of the son known	identity of the son unknown
tameness	savagery
civilization	bestiality

The Cecrops myth is about marriage. In the commentary the correlates of the human pole represent the male culture created by marriage. Those of the bestial pole inform the threat to it from unrestrained sex and so are identified with women. The degree to which this thinking is male-oriented is demonstrated by the last correlate of the bestial pole. Women are supposed to mate like beasts; the ancient scholar failed to realize that in mating with them the men are as bestial.

Plato's Escape from Marriage

Matriarchy comes to an end with Cecrops's institution of patriarchal marriage—namely, the yoking of one woman to one man. In his ideal state Plato eliminates marriage for the Guardians, men and women bred and trained to rule and defend the state.[21] There emerges a view of women in society so similar to that of the mythic matriarchy that it comes near to proving the nonhistoricity of matriarchy as evidenced at least by myths.

Plato begins by asking how the principle governing the Guard-ians—"friends have things in common"—applies to their women and children. Before answering this question, however, he digresses to discuss the nature of females.

> *Socrates*. Do we think that female guard dogs should join in guarding whatever the males guard and hunt with them and do everything in common with them? or, do we think that they should remain inside as if incapacitated by the bearing and rearing of pups, and that the males work and have all the care of the flocks?
> *Glaucon*. Everything in common, except that we treat the fe-males as weaker and the males as stronger.
> *Socrates*. Is it possible to use any animal for the same purpose as another if you do not give it the same food and training?
> *Glaucon*. No, it is not.
> *Socrates*. If we use women for the same purposes as men, they must be taught the same things.[22]

Women of the Guardians must be reared and trained in the same manner as the men because their duties are the same as the men's. Such differences as do exist between the sexes, like those between guard dogs, do not pertain to their role as Guardians. Thus women may be rulers. Plato then returns to the first question about the principle.

> *Socrates*. The following law derives from the principle [gov-erning Guardians] and all that has been said before it:
> all women shall be held in common by all men, no woman shall live together with a man, the children shall be in com-mon, and neither parent shall know his own child nor the child the parent.[23]

The resemblance to pre-Cecropian matriarchy is obvious. Plato wanted to abolish marriage and the family because he considered them a source of multiple social evils. The family divided the com-munity into individual and exclusive competing units. By holding women and children in common, the Guardians would be free from the distractions of maintaining a household and having to find money for the wife and servants. Matriarchy and utopia would liberate women from patriarchal marriage—the one to justify it, the other to escape its evils.

The "women question" was under discussion among the intelligentsia at Athens during the late fifth and early fourth centuries. Aristophanes' comedies, *Lysistrata* (411 B.C.) and *Ecclesiaszusae* [*Women in the Assembly*] (392 B.C.), as well as Euripides' later plays, reflect interest in women. Socrates believed in their intellectual ability. Plato probably heard Socrates speaking on the subject, but Plato is no feminist.[24] His Guardian women, despite their position, are selected for the men, and they are bestowed as prizes, though not possessions, on distinguished warriors. Only women are said to be held in common, though the same is true of men. Plato's views of women follow from his argument and perhaps from disinterest in their lives.

Clytemnestra's Repudiation of Marriage

In the *Agamemnon,* marriage is violated first by Agamemnon and then by Clytemnestra. War and deliberation, the spheres proper to the male, are turned against the family, the female sphere. Clytemnestra retaliates by repudiating marriage and usurping Agamemnon's rule, and the loss of the distinctions that constitute gender roles ensues. Since Agamemnon is king as well as husband, familial chaos engulfs the social and cosmic planes.

The *Agamemnon* opens with a watchman on the roof of the royal house waiting for the beacon signaling the fall of Troy. The audience quickly learns, to its surprise, that he is not Aegisthus's man as in the Homeric tradition. Clytemnestra has put him there; her "man-counseling expectant heart wields the power" within the house. When Agamemnon sailed for Troy, he left her behind as his regent, and the Chorus of Argive elders recognizes her authority on that basis. But, as R. P. Winnington-Ingram has pointed out, she has seized power and counsel for herself.[25] The first choral ode gives a reason: Agamemnon sacrificed her daughter, Iphigenia, to appease Artemis's anger and to get favorable winds for his journey.[26] The events culminating in the sacrifice are these: Paris, while a guest in Menelaus's house, steals his host's wife, Helen. Zeus, god of hosts, is affronted and sends Agamemnon and Menelaus as avengers upon Paris and the Trojans. For an omen of their success, Zeus's eagles tear apart a pregnant hare. Artemis, kind and lovely goddess of the beasts, is indignant over the break in the stream of life caused by the premature deaths of the hare and her unborn young. She begrudges the eagles their feasting and, hemming in the fleet at Aulis in Boeotia, gives Agamemnon the choice of sacrificing his daughter or abandoning the expedition. Agamemnon does not try to palliate the unnaturalness of the act he contemplates:

> Not to be persuaded is a heavy doom, but heavy too if I
> slaughter my child, the delight of my house, polluting with
> streams of maiden's gore the father's hands beside the altar.

But he asks himself, "Which of these is without evils? How can I become a deserter, losing my alliance? To desire the sacrifice that stays the winds and the maiden's blood passionately with passion is right." His language conceals the fact that the passion for the sacrifice is his; to long for the sacrifice of his daughter is *themis*—that is, "right" or "in the order of things."[27] He dares to take her life as "an aid for a war that avenges a woman and as a preliminary sacrifice for the ships."

Both Clytemnestra and Iphigenia are under Agamemnon's mastery as head of the household. Aeschylus poses the question, "What would happen if the mother resisted her husband's right to dispose of their daughter as he wished in promoting the well-being of his household?" His answer is Clytemnestra's matriarchy. Though Aeschylus does not condone the act, he represents it as no more than an extreme of the father's mastery, which, had Clytemnestra remained within marriage and obedient to her husband's will, would have been overlooked in the success at Troy. The Chorus tells him on his return:[28]

At that time you were equipping the army for Helen's sake—I
will not hide it—you were not wielding the tiller of good
sense well by restoring courage to dying men from sacrifice.
But now from the depths of my mind and as a true friend I
am delighted for those who have successfully accomplished
their labor.

Its approval follows from society's dependence upon the daring of
men, whose excesses were tolerated in victory.

The myth of Demeter and Persephone also is about the tensions created by a father's mastery over his daughter and thus
provides a contrast. Zeus, unbeknown to Demeter, gives their
daughter, Persephone, in marriage to his brother, Hades. Hades
arises from the earth, seizes her while she is picking flowers, and
carries her to the underworld. When Demeter discovers what has
happened, a savage grief comes over her, and she leaves Olympus
for earth, eventually arriving at Eleusis. There she tries to console
herself for the loss of her daughter by tending the king's son.
When that fails, she causes a barrenness over the land, and no
crops grow. She would have destroyed mankind, thus depriving
the gods of the savour of sacrifice, had Zeus not intervened. An
agreement is reached whereby Persephone is allowed to spend part
of the year with her mother. During the remaining months she
resides in the underworld with her husband as his respected
queen.[29]

The myth portrays another answer to the question asked by
Aeschylus. The relationship between mother and daughter is a
temporary one; it must yield to marriage and separation. Per-
sephone-the-daughter inevitably becomes Demeter-the-mother, the
biological wheel upon which male society and human life depend.
On the other hand, the mother must consent to the marriage, the
daughter must be given away and not taken in rape, and both must
be rewarded for their sacrifice. The violence of the husband and
the heedlessness of the father are chastised as the males are forced
to recognize their dependency upon females for their fertility.

Throughout her resistance, however, Demeter remains within the female sphere, while Clytemnestra exceeds hers by usurping male power and counsel, creating a matriarchy imagined by Aeschylus to be the reversal of the structures of male order—marriage, language, and sacrifice.

Clytemnestra assumes the husband's place by introducing Aegisthus into the house at the hearth, and like the virgin bride, he enters it for primarily sexual purposes. Clytemnestra dominates her liaison with Aegisthus, who, again like a woman, is a stay-at-home who remained behind from the Trojan War. Once marriage is abolished in this fashion, animal bestiality is let loose, which, as shown by the Cecrops myth, is synonymous with female rule. Aeschylus conveys the bestiality of their arrangements through animal imagery: Aegisthus is a wolf mating with Clytemnestra, a lion.[30] Clytemnestra further reverses marital roles by feminizing Agamemnon and forcing him to yield to her in their "battle" at the doors of the house.[31] Consequently, her marriage is not a civilized union but, in Aeschylus's imagery, is a congress of lions. Even in imagery it is against nature: when Cassandra cries, "Keep the bull from the cow," it is to protect him, the bull, figure of male strength and fertility.[32] Most heinous of all, Clytemnestra kills her husband, an act ultimately judged far more infamous than Agamemnon's murder of his daughter. All natural and cultural bonds joining man and woman and distinguishing their union from bestial promiscuity are severed by Clytemnestra.

The goal of marriage is the propagation of children, the son as heir and a daughter to exchange in marriage. The husband is the "straight pillar of the lofty roof"; he is its defender and bearer of the generative phallus. No matter how he satisfies Clytemnestra by kindling "the fire at [her] hearth," Aegisthus is a usurper in another's place, unable to beget legitimate children.[33] With the father dead, the existing children are in limbo. The son, Orestes, banished from his father's house as a child, is deprived of his throne and inheritance. Electra, the daughter, without a father to give her away, cannot be married. According to the law of classical Athens, the background of the play, Electra would have passed into the mastery of her father's brother or of her brother at his coming of age, but Menelaus is lost at sea and Orestes is in exile. She is confined to her paternal home, barren and deprived of her right to a husband and children.[34] Finally, the role of the Greek wife was to protect whatever her husband brought into the house. Clytemnestra ostentatiously squanders Agamemnon's wealth by strewing the ground with rich tapestries for him to tread.[35]

Humans communicate with other humans through language; it distinguishes them from the animals who have mere voice. "Speech," according to Aristotle, "has the purpose of clarifying the useful and the harmful and so also the just and unjust."[36] In Aeschylus's mythmaking, language is the province of men. The Chorus compliments Clytemnestra by saying, "You speak sensibly like a prudent man." Apollo gave Cassandra speech that prophesies, but she reneged on her promise to submit to him. As her punishment, she foresees the future, but her language fails to communicate anything not already known.[37] The constructive word is male. On Clytemnestra's lips language is not an instrument of communication, for it requires "clear interpreters" to decode its hidden message. Deceitful, ruinously seductive, it is utterly beyond Agamemnon's understanding. In a scene discussed in Chapter Five Clytemnestra wheedles him into playing the woman and hides her situation with Aegisthus long enough to slay her husband. And when she does the deed, her words and actions transform murder into blasphemous sacrifice.

Sacrifice distinguishes men who offer it from the gods who receive it and the animals who are offered. In the common view sacrifice was man's way of bestowing gifts upon the gods.[38] Clytemnestra sends them the present of Agamemnon's blood; she sacrifices the sacrificer, a confusion marked by her reference to Agamemnon as *teleios anēr*. *Teleios* denotes the man (*anēr*) as "in authority" and "sexually mature," but also as "a perfect sacrifical victim."[39] Moreover, Clytemnestra nullifies sacrifice as a means of removing violence from the community. Sacrifices appeased divine wrath and through purifications mediated disputes between men.[40] Violence that would be vented against another member of society was turned against a sacrificial victim. Being an animal, the victim had no social standing and no one to avenge it; the violence ended with its death. But both Agamemnon and Clytemnestra choose a victim who has an avenger. Their acts transform ritualized slaughter into murder, thus introducing violence into the family and community. The difference between them is that Agamemnon's act is an iniquitous extreme of a father's mastery, something men can overlook without condoning because it is done in support of the system of male rule. Clytemnestra's act confounds the distinction between human sacrificer and animal victim, thereby eliminating the distinction between men and animals, overthrowing male rule, and opening up an unbreachable gap between men and their gods.

As a result of Clytemnestra's repudiation of marriage, chaos emanates beyond the house to engulf the cosmos. As king, Agamemnon is the focal point of the state's relationship with nature.[41] With his death, the worlds of nature and community are no longer in harmony. The use of images of withered and dying vegetation, of preternaturally adverse weather, and of things normally beneficent (such as light and motherhood) to connote evil expresses their discontinuity. The sea, for example, "flowers with corpses of men."[42] Clytemnestra upsets the workings of nature by killing the king and corrupting the sacred marriage of Sky and Earth:

> He fell [she boasts] and shot forth his life. Breathing out a spurting slaughter of bloody gore, he hits me with a dark shower of bloody dew. In it I pleasure no less than the new-sown field in the joy sent by Zeus at the birthing of the buds.[43]

The union of Sky and Earth through Sky's fertilizing rain was a sacred model of the reproductive process based on male dominance. When Clytemnestra glories in the shower of Agamemnon's blood, it is Zeus's fluid which now signals death, not life. She is earth mother of a harvest of death, "a hellish mother raging with sacrifices, a curse breathing implacably against her kin."[44] Her act of repudiating marriage destroys order throughout the cosmos. In her Aeschylus has portrayed one consequence of the female outside marriage—matriarchy made of the negation of male order through the reversal of patriarchal institutions and values.

·CHAPTER 3·

Amazon Customs and the Patriarchy

AMAZON SOCIETY is an *ethnos gynaikokratoumenon,* "a nation where women have the power," a matriarchy, and as such it is a

mirror image of patriarchy. We have already discussed evidence for the attitudes, beliefs, and institutions reflecting the sexual asymmetry of male dominance at Athens. But that evidence which is so strongly suggestive of what the sexes were supposed to do—evidence of their gender roles—comes from words written and vases painted by men, and should a woman speak, she sounds through a male voice. No Sappho exists in our purview of Athens. To what extent personal temperament, economic circumstances, and class status altered the pattern prescribed for gender roles is nearly unknown. The sources dwell on the exceptional, the scandalous. This circumstance, bedeviling for the history of Athenian women as individuals rather than as Woman the group or construct, does not hinder the present study. In this chapter Amazon customs are compared with the system of cultural norms and practices supporting Athenian patriarchy. The Amazons' customs reverse the ideal or model—not the reality—according to which citizen men and women were supposed to conduct their lives. And for this there is sufficient and more solid evidence.

40

ON THE SOURCES FOR AMAZON CUSTOMS

From the classical period, as we have seen, the Amazon myth concerns primarily Heracles' Ninth Labor, Theseus's rape of an Amazon, and the defense of Athens. Little is handed down about the customs of the Amazons, for which we must turn to post-classical sources, among them, Diodorus Siculus (first century B.C.) and Strabo (first century B.C.–first century A.D.). If the present study were directed exclusively at the myth, the chronological dis-crepancy would not be a problem. But an attempt is being made here to locate the myth in the context of classical Athenian so-ciety, so the issue must be faced. Details were added at various times—the accretions of Pherecydes and Hellanicus are examples—but the general outline of the myth, its themes, and its motifs were established during the classical period. Although the Ama-zons' control of the public sphere, for example, or their antipathy to male babies may be variously imagined, both situations are con-sistent with the myth and are assumptions of the classical era. But Lysias's mythmaking, discussed in Chapter One, and Herodotus's account of the Sauromatians' Amazon ancestry, to which we now return, alone prove the case, for they have been formed by revers-ing patriarchal customs.[1]

Sauromatian women rode horses and handled the bow along with the men. Herodotus explains this by tracing their origin to the union of Scythians with Amazons captured by the Greeks after their defeat on the Thermodon. Put into ships, the Amazons rise up against the Greeks and slay them. Since they are ignorant of sailing, they drift until landing in the territory of the Scythians.[2] Here they steal horses and live by plundering. The Scythians first fight with them, but after they find out their sex, they send their youngest men to court them. The men refrain from attacking but follow behind them, retreating whenever the Amazons turn to attack. Eventually a Scythian happens upon an Amazon alone, and when she does not repel his advances, they have intercourse. The couple agrees to meet on the next day and to bring a friend; in this way "the Scythians tame the rest of the Amazons."

The men after a while wish to go home to parents and possessions, but the Amazons refuse:

> We would not be able to live with your women, for our customs are not the same as theirs. We practice the bow and javelin and ride horses. We have not learned women's work. Your women do none of these things; they do women's tasks, staying in the wagons and not going on the hunt or anywhere. We could not get along with them. But if you want to have us as your wives and to seem most fair toward us, go to your parents and get your share of their possessions. When you return, let's live by ourselves.

When the men return with their portion of their fathers' estates, the Amazons profess to being afraid of living near those whose land they have plundered. They want to move away. Their husbands consent, and the couples leave Scythia.

It is noteworthy, first of all, that the myth is about marriage, not combat or war. Several significant elements have come about by reversing the customs of patriarchal marriage. The Scythians are said to have "tamed" the Amazons. Previously they must have been wild, a condition whose meaning is clarified by the Cecrops myth and by the common view of marriage as the antithesis of animal abandon.[3] Sexual relations in Greek marriage took place within the house; Amazons mate outside. Like Greek women, the Scythians (who stand for Greek women) are "very young" when they marry. Also like Greek women, a dowry taken from their fathers is given to their spouses as a token of their "fairness" toward them. In Greek marriage, the bride came with a dowry, one carefully calculated to show her father's esteem for the groom.[4] The Scythians, like Greek brides, leave their fathers' houses to live with their spouses in a place of the latter's choosing. Finally, consistent with later sources are the Amazons' control of the public sphere of hunting and war and their rejection of the tasks done by the Scythian women, who, like Greek women, are confined to the wagon-house.

For later writers the question is one of fixing their sources in the classical period. Even then we cannot always be certain of what they took from a source or whether they used it directly or through an intermediary. Diodorus Siculus wrote a history of all the known peoples of the world. *The Library* is a scissors-and-paste compilation of earlier works. For the Libyan Amazons, Diodorus says, he used Dionysius Scytobrachion, "Leather Arm," a novelist living in Alexandria during the second century B.C.[5] Dionysius composed mythological romances by stringing together myths in a grand synthesis. He connected the story of the *Odyssey* with the adventures of Jason and the Argonauts, for instance, by making Odysseus's father, Laertes, an Argonaut. His books won for him the reputation of a swindler and a nickname denoting his endurance in writing out copious details. He used, or at least cited, the works of "the ancients, both mythographers and poets."[6] His Amazons are unique, not for their customs, but for their residence in Libya and for fighting the gorgons and the inhabitants of Atlantis.

The geographer Strabo says in the passage quoted below that he consulted ancient authors, among them Hecataeus, Herodotus, and Hellanicus. He regarded them all as makers of myth, not history. Strabo used extensively the historian Ephorus (fourth century B.C.), a pupil of Isocrates who came to Athens from Cyme in Ionia. Ephorus wrote a history of his native city which traced its founding to an Amazon; he also wrote a history of Greece. He used Hecataeus, Herodotus, and, for the earlier period, Hellanicus in particular.[7] References in later writers confirm that Ephorus recounted the Amazon myth in his history of Greece.

A compelling indication of the consistency of the Amazon myth from the classical version to those of Diodorus and Strabo is this statement by Strabo:

A peculiar thing has happened in the account of the Amazons. Other accounts keep the mythical and historical elements distinguished. The ancient, deceitful and monstrous, they call myths, whereas history aims at the truth, whether ancient or modern, and the monstrous has either no place or only an infrequent one. Concerning the Amazons, however, the same things are said now as in ancient times, things that are monstrous and beyond belief. Who could believe that an army or city or nation of women could be organized without men? or, that not only could it be organized but even could attack a foreign country, subdue its neighbors as far as present-day Ionia, and launch an expedition across the sea as far as Attica? It is tantamount to saying that the men of that day were women, and the women were men. Yet the same things are being said now about them, a circumstance that augments the peculiarity regarding them and our belief in the ancient authors rather than the modern ones.[8]

Strabo believed that myths were composed of wondrous and monstrous elements and a historical core. The poet grafted the former upon a historical truth just as when "some man pours gold around silver."[9] The wondrous and monstrous elements aim at pleasure, the charm that draws men to learn from myths, or at fear, which deters them from evil. Pleasurable wonders include the deeds of Heracles; fearful ones are stories of divine punishment. But the mythmaker, whether poet or lawgiver, does not fabricate a tale of pure fiction. A historical kernel, the truth the myth seeks to explain, can be extracted. In the case of the Amazon myth, according to Strabo, the separation of truth from the monstrous failed. That failure indicates that the myth was told by later writers in the same way as by earlier ones, even though it entailed a "monstrous" reversal of gender roles—women who do what men do.

REVERSALS AND OPPOSITIONS IN AMAZON CUSTOMS

What follows is an examination of Amazon customs and the oppositions informing them as the reversals of patriarchal customs. It is a first step in decoding the myth, emptying it of its patriarchal content. If one were to remove everything Western from Japanese culture, for example, much that is authentically Japanese would remain. In the case of the Amazon myth, however, this process will show that apart from Athenian patriarchy the Amazon has no substance. The attempt to separate fact from fancy failed because without the reversals there is nothing.[10]

Inside/Outside

A fundamental polarity of Athenian patriarchy is inside/outside. Associated with women was the indoors—the inner domain of womb and home. "The outer door of the house is the boundary for the free woman."[11] Segregated from women of other households, with only female relatives by marriage and slaves for company, women tended to the domestic chores of running the house for their husbands. The outdoors had a masculine connotation; its attributes—movement, strength, endurance, wisdom, toil, and danger—were the antitheses of the feminine indoors. Men left the dark confines of the house for war, politics, business, and pleasure, activities entered into mostly under the brilliant Mediterranean sky.[12]

The Athenian Xenophon, in a treatise on the management of the household, provides a classic description of this opposition. It is in the form of the gentleman-farmer Ischomachus's instructions to his wife on her duties. His pedantic, condescending tone is due to his bride's age; she was not yet fifteen.

> Now in my opinion, wife, the gods seem to have devised the pair called female and male with particular insight that it be most advantageous to itself for the good of its common enterprise. First of all, so that the generations of living things might not fail, the pair lies with one another in begetting children. Secondly, from the pair is provided, for humans at any rate, the means of acquiring those who will attend their old age. Next, the way of life for humans is not, as it is for cattle, in the outdoors, but there is need for a roof. That is clear. Certainly for humans who intend to have something

to bring into the house, there is needed someone to do the
outdoor work. Plowing, sowing, planting, pasturing, all these
are outdoor occupations. From them come the necessities
of life. There is need, in turn, when these are brought into the
house, for someone to watch over and tend to the proper
occupations of the house. The care of new-born children
needs a house; the preparation of bread from grain needs a
house, as does the making of clothes from wool. Since both
occupations, those inside and those outside, need work
and attention, the god, as it seems to me, made nature accord-
ingly: the woman's for indoor occupations and the man's
for outdoor ones. He made the body and spirit of the man
more able to overcome cold, heat, travel, and military service.
Thus he assigned to him the outdoor occupations. Since he
endowed the woman by nature with a body less able to overcome the rigors of cold, heat, travel, and military service,
the god seems to me to have assigned to her the indoor tasks.
Knowing that he had endowed her by nature and assigned her
the rearing of new-born children, he also apportioned to her
more affection for new-born babies than to the man. Since he
also assigned to the woman the watching over what was
brought into the house, and since he realized that for guarding
it was no loss if the soul be timid, the god apportioned a
greater amount of timidity to the woman than to the man.
On the other hand, knowing that there will be need for the
one who has the outdoor occupations to act in defense of
them, the god apportioned to the man the greater amount of
courage. [13]

Correlated with inside/outside are the oppositions of love
for children/strength to endure cold, etc., and timidity/courage.
The arrangement of gender roles organized by these antitheses,
Ischomachus assures his wife, was grounded in nature, given by the
gods, and confirmed by law. [14] The Amazons reverse the polarity:
they are avatars of the outdoors.

Beside the Thermodon River, they say, was a nation ruled by
women where women shared the obligations of war equally
with men. One woman, who possessed the royal power,
excelled the rest in courage and strength. She organized and
trained an army of women and subdued some of her neighbors. Growing in bravery and fame, she campaigned unceas-
ingly against nearby peoples. Her fortunes prospered, and
she took on lofty aspirations. She called herself the daughter
of Ares and assigned to the men the spinning of wool and
the domestic work of the women. She established laws according to which the women went to the contests of war, and
humility and slavery were fastened on the men. They mutilated the legs and arms of the males who were born, rendering
them useless for war. They seared the right breast of the
female infants in order to prevent it from swelling out and
being in the way when their bodies matured. For this reason
the nations of Amazons received their name.

They say that in the western parts of Libya, on the borders
of the known world, was a nation ruled by women which
pursued a way of life not like our own. It was the custom for
women to toil in war and to be obligated for an enlistment
in the army. During this period they remained virgins; after
their years of service they approached men for procreation of
children. The magistracies and affairs of state were administered by women. The men, like our married women, spent
their time in the house tending to the orders of their wives.
They had no share in the army or magistracies nor any say in
public affairs from which they might become presumptuous
and attack the women. When the babies were born, they
handed them over to the men, who fed them with milk and
other boiled foods suitable to the ages of the infants.

The Amazons do their several tasks by themselves [i.e., apart
from men], the plowing, planting, pasturing of cattle, and, in

particular, the raising of horses. The bravest make much of hunting from horseback and of training for war.[15]

Among the Amazons the outside is female. The women go hunting, exercise in the open, and ride off to war; the men stay at home and cook for the babies. To the women belong strength and the prerogatives attained by strength, the magistracies and affairs of state. Prohibitions on men—forbidding them to bear arms and to govern—together with the maiming of infant males, are equivalent to the Greek woman's disenfranchisement and to the timidity installed, according to Ischomachus, in the female nature by god.

Also correlated with inside/outside is movement/rest. The Greek woman's mobility was confined, except for religious obligations, by the courtyard gate. (Exceptions must have been numerous, but such was the ideal.) Greek men propagandized women's place by commissioning vases whose paintings depicted them at home at their chores. T. B. L. Webster points to the dramatic rise in the number of paintings of women alone, without men, on vases used by women in the early classical and classical periods, particularly in Attica:

> Whatever vases women had bought or been given for their
> own purposes before, they had not found on vases pictures of
> their own occupations in such quantities before. The vase-
> painters were meeting a new demand. When one thinks of the
> restrictions on women's life in Athens, it seems probable
> that the demand came from men rather than from the women
> themselves. The vases were more often presents from men
> to women (or offerings at women's tombs) than purchases by
> women.[16]

Although we hear of Amazon cities, we rarely hear of Amazons under a roof.[17] They are figments of the outdoors, and, like Greek men, they are on the move. Movement is one meaning of the horse, whose opposite, lack of movement, is represented by the crippling of males. Movement is also one aspect of the meaning of the Amazon's lost breast.

The sources widely report that Amazons have a single breast. While the left one is retained for nursing, the right one is stunted by searing or removed in some fashion lest it impede the throwing of the javelin.[18] To the Greeks the condition accounted for the Amazons' name—*a-* (no) + *mazos* (breast)—but it is more likely that the name accounted for the condition. Etymology, however, is not all there is to Amazon monomastia. Why, in analyzing the name, did single-breastedness seem appropriate? One reason is movement—not only movement as freedom to hurl the javelin but movement as freedom from nursing. Another is that the warmth and comfort of the mother and the vital nourishment of the child center on the breast. It is the mother's last resort in appealing to her adult child to obey her.[19] As much as possible, Amazons are released from maternal attachments.

In view of what has been said about the movement of Amazons as opposed to the condition of rest of Greek women, Strabo's description of the Amazons' sedentary ways—plowing, planting, raising livestock—seems out of place. It is, and it is not. Agriculture ties Amazons to the soil and so denies them mobility. But what governs the depiction of Amazon customs in the myths is not consistency from one version to another. New elements were readily added; when drawn together, they may contradict one another. What governs the image of the Amazon, however, is the logic of its structure—in this case, the reversal of inside/outside. Agriculture, the production of grain for bread and grapes for wine, is an outdoor activity of men. Ischomachus makes this clear to his wife. When Strabo attributes agriculture to the Amazons, he adds one aspect to the structure of reversal while contradicting another. Diodorus, as will be seen, denies the Amazons agriculture in accordance with a difference opposition.

Weaponry

Weaponry in the language of the myth is at first neutral. In the epic and on black-figure vases, Amazons bear the same arms as the Greeks.[20] With the assimilation of Amazons and Persians, weaponry becomes a value-laden code of oppositions.

Heracles and the Homeric warrior fought "in front of the fore-most" for individual glory. The shield each carried was for his own protection. During the archaic and classical periods the mainstay of land warfare was the *hoplitēs,* "he of the *hoplon* or shield." The hoplite was a citizen who paid for his own armor and fought in a formation with other citizens against similar formations. His shield was designed for this style of fighting. It was secured to the left arm by two straps, one in the center and the other near the rim. The man inserted his arm in the center strap to the elbow and gripped the outer strap with his hand. This arrangement of straps extended half of the shield beyond the wearer's left side while ex-posing his right side. That meant that each man protected the man on his left and looked for protection to the man on his right.[21] The safety of all required the courage of each man to stand beside his fellows. "O young men," Tyrtaeus exhorts his fellow Spartans, "remain beside one another and fight. Do not begin shameful flight or panic. . . . Let man stand firm and remain, fixed with both feet on the ground, biting his lips."[22]

Hoplite fighting, the *polis* at war, manifests the same priority as the *polis* at peace: the individual in partnership with others, the whole having precedence over its parts.[23] It was the warfare that won Marathon and that came to be ennobled as befitting men of honor.[24] It demanded close quarters with the enemy, strength to support the armor and wield the thrusting spear, and, most of all, the courage to stand and fight man-to-man.

Amazons as depicted on vases carry both heavy and light armor; the literary tradition favors the latter.[25] Nonhoplite armor mani-fests speed, mobility, distance from the enemy, individuality, and foreignness. Amazons carry a moon-shaped, hide-covered shield and wear a cap of leather. They are often dressed in Persian trou-sers. Their main weapon is the curved Scythian bow, though they also use the ax, spear, and javelin. They appear on foot and on horseback on the vases; literary sources prefer horseback.

The bow was reviled from Homeric times as a coward's weapon because with it one could kill from a safe distance.[26] On the other hand, it was a menacing feature of Persian warfare. The Athenians at Marathon ran under the weight of their armor to engage the enemy before they could let loose their missiles. Their fusillade before the battle of Thermopylae, it was said, would shut out the sun. So striking was the bow that the Greeks made it the Persian weapon *par excellence,* even though the Persians themselves relied on the spear. Faced with archers, unless supported by their own long-range troops, hoplites were vulnerable and thrown on the defensive.[27] In the language of the weapons code, then, the bow is ambivalent. It denotes a mode of fighting that is both beneath a Greek and terrifying to him—a suitable weapon for an Amazon, a woman yet a redoubtable foe.

In the code of weaponry the horse denotes a quick escape without concern for others. It may have another meaning in the context of wealth. Horses were expensive to buy and maintain and so were synonymous with wealthy aristocrats. Cavalry was the fighting mode of rich oligarchies; in poetry a mare was a metaphor for a rich woman. Perhaps the defeat of the horse-riding Amazons struck a chord among some citizens as the defeat of wealth and noble birth.[28]

A weapon consciously regarded as foreign was the ax, the single-edged *sagaris* or the double-edged *pelekus.* The opposition of spear/ax is implied in the response of the Spartan hostages to the Persian Hydanes: "If you should experience liberty, you would advise us to fight for it not with spears only but even with axes."[29] That is to say, once the Persian tasted freedom, he would become like a Greek and fight for it not just with the ordinary weapon of the Greek, the spear, but with its antithesis, the ax. To what extent, if any, its foreignness was accentuated by its being a religious symbol in Crete and Lydia is immeasurable. Perhaps it had particular meaning (or gained it from the wall paintings) as a woman's weapon against men. Clytemnestra, realizing her imminent death, inexplicably cries out for a "man-wearying" ax.[30]

As a code in the language of the myth, Amazon weaponry is a reversal of Greek arms. It reflects the Greek view of the Persian wars as a victory of free men over slaves and proves the superiority of the principle of the whole over those who, because of their enslavement, thought first of themselves.[31] A final note: Hellanicus described the Amazons as "a golden-shielded, silver-axed host." Wealth is an attribute not of Amazons but of Persians. One thousand of Xerxes' elite troops, the Immortals, were distinguished by golden pomegranates at the lower ends of their spears, and the other nine thousand by silver ones.[32] Aeschylus, in the *Persians* (472 B.C.), contrasts the splendor of Persian gold and wealth with the humility of Xerxes' return home. Hellanicus, in his description, may be alluding to Persian display.

Control of Marriage and Reproductivity

Control of marriage and reproductivity was a pillar of Athenian patriarchy. All her life the citizen-woman was under the mastery of a man—her father, her husband, her nearest male relative. (Not to be so was the mark of an alien or a prostitute.) He met with the groom and arranged her betrothal, pledging her in marriage. She was young and had little say in the matter. The philosophers recommended eighteen years as the best age for marriage; many women were given away earlier, notably when the father died and there was no male heir. Every precaution was taken to publicize the arrangements, for there were no city halls or licenses. Legitimacy depended upon witnesses, so much so that the failure to have enough witnesses could provide *prima facie* evidence against the validity of the marriage.[33] Except when the bride was pledged as a child, the wedding followed directly upon her betrothal. Cohabitation consummated the marriage; the Greek word for being married is *synoikein*, "to share a house." Once married, a woman was expected to be modest and sexually undemanding, even cool, her *raison d'être* being the procreation of children.[34] The life that lay before her may be glimpsed from Plutarch's prescriptions on the ideal in his *Advice to the Bride and Groom*:

> The modest wife ought to be most conspicuous in her husband's company and stay in the house and hide when he is away.

Herodotus was mistaken when he said a woman takes off her modesty along with her clothes. Quite the opposite, she puts on modesty in their place, and the husband and wife show the greatest modesty as a token of their very great love for each other.

Every activity in the house is carried out with modesty by both in agreement but displays the leadership and preferences of the husband.

The wife ought not to have any feelings of her own but join with her husband in his moods whether serious, playful, thoughtful, or joking.

Should a man in private life be without control or guidance in his pleasures and commit some indiscretion with a prostitute or servant girl, the wife should not take it hard or be angry, reasoning that because of his respect for her, he does not include her in his drunken parties, excesses, and wantonness with other women.

The wife ought not to have friends of her own but share her husband's in common with him.

Not gold, not gems, not scarlet, make a woman more proper, but whatever invests her appearance with dignity, discipline, and shame.

I think the modest woman has the greatest need for charming her husband so that . . . she may live with him pleasantly and not be irritable because she is modest.

She ought to speak to her husband or through her husband and not be disgruntled if, like the fluteplayer, she utters sounds through the tongue of another.[35]

The Amazons shun marriage in the Greek sense and display none of the modesty proper to an Athenian woman. Despite their hostility to men, they like them and arouse them sexually, but control of reproductivity belongs to women in the Amazon myth.

The men who tend the babies are no better than slaves, and slaves are not a source of citizen-children in Greek or Amazon society.[36] It is Greeks the Amazons are wont to arouse. Theseus had to sneak away to avoid their advances. In Herodotus's account one Amazon consents to the advances of a Scythian, and things develop from there. Another tries to seduce Heracles; Penthesilea captures Achilles' love even as she lies dying beneath his sword.[37]

Strabo gives the most extensive version of the mating practices:

> They have two special months when they go up to the neigh-
> boring mountain on the border with the Gargarians. The
> men go up there, following an ancient custom, to offer sacri-
> fice with the women and to mate with them for the sake
> of begetting children. Unions occur unseen [*aphanōs*] and in
> the dark between whatever man happens by with whatever
> woman happens by. Having impregnated them, the Gargarians
> send the women away.[38]

There is nothing to this but reversals. A roof was for Xenophon's Ischomachus a *sine qua non* of the married couple; Amazon unions take place outside like those of the cattle in his antithesis. Athenian marriages were arranged and witnessed, planned, and publicized. Amazon unions take place by chance, any man with any woman. They occur unseen and hence unknown, an association present in the Greek word *aphanōs* (unseen). Unlike the constancy that constitutes an Athenian marriage. Amazon unions are one-shot affairs. The myth says nothing about any Amazon's remaining with the same Gargarian during the mating season.

Children

Children in patriarchal society are under the mastery of their father. Although all Greek sons were valued as defenders of the house and city, the first-born was prized. As his father's heir, he perpetuated the paternal line and kept alive the past line through ancestor worship. On him was imposed the burden of the survival of the house. Strict surveillance of the bride's virginity and the wife's chastity was intended to ensure that the son she bore was her husband's. Otherwise his family worship and citizen's role might be contaminated by nonmembers. That anxiety governed the existence of the Athenian woman.[39] Daughters, on the other hand, were a drain on the resources of the house, and a father would want no more than he could dower. Generally less well fed and less well educated, daughters were transferred by marriage to another house as soon as possible.[40]

In Amazon society legitimacy is based on blood. Unlike the Athenian father, the Amazon mother could not doubt the parenthood of the child she carried, and the father was of no consequence. Thus, the precautions of the Greek marriage are opposed by the element of chance, and the primacy of the sexes is reversed. Girls are valued; boys are banished, mutilated, or killed.[41] Strabo's version of the fate of boys is a reversal of the notion of the valued child, which negates the religious link between father and son:

> The women keep whatever female children are born, while they take the males to the Gargarians to bring up. Each man claims one as his own, believing it to be his son on account of his ignorance.[42]

Religion of the Amazons

The mechanism of reversal holds true for the religion of the Amazons. Their gods are the berserker Ares; the Phrygian Magna Mater, Cybele; and Artemis, under several cult titles. Directed toward war and fertility, their religion is practiced in orgiastic rites and is dominated by the female.[43] Women were prominent in Athenian state agricultural festivals, but in those rites they mediated between the earth and a community dependent upon fertility but dominated by men. Amazons treat with the god on their own behalf, and their gods are non-Hellenic, savage, and barbarian.[44]

Amazon Homelands

The myth gives several locations for the Amazons' homeland. Homer placed them in Lycia and in Phrygia on the Sangarius River.

His attribution of the tomb on the Trojan plain to the Amazon Myrine, an etiology similar to the ones assigning the names of Ionian cities to Amazons, alludes to an earlier tradition—their presence along the Ionian coast. Arctinus (eight century B.C.?), in the *Aethiopis,* a continuation of the *Iliad,* spoke of the Thracian Penthesilea. The most celebrated location of the Amazon homeland is the southern shore of the Black Sea on the Thermodon River. According to Aeschylus, the Amazons arrived there from Colchis, which he placed (incorrectly) north of the Black Sea around Lake Maeotis. Other locations are further east in the foothills of the Caucasus Mountains north of Albania and in the south in African Libya.[45]

The first thing to notice about Amazon homelands is that they are outside Greece. Even in myth, the inversion of the cosmos— that is, the reversal of the patriarchy that informs Amazon customs —is not admitted into the fatherland. When Amazons do invade Greece, they are killed; only their graves remain. Amazons dwell on the edge of the known world. Diodorus specifically locates one group "in the western parts of Libya on the ends of the inhabited world."[46] As the known world expanded, Amazons were moved outward from Ionia to Phrygia and from the Thermodon River to Lake Maeotis and the Caucasus Mountains. The edge of the *oikoumenē* (inhabited world) is literally and metaphorically the frontier between civilization and savagery. Less a place than an idea, it expresses spatially the breakdown of differences, of the categories used to define culture and to distinguish it from bestiality below and divinity above. When the extremes are blurred, the middle, the human condition as it is, is lost, the poles collapse into each other, and the monstrous, or perhaps the wondrous, invades the cosmos. As a place, the frontier is the *coincidentia oppositorum* (the falling in together of the opposites), and is thus populated with both subhuman and suprahuman figures: Centaurs, gorgons, the Hesperides, the Hyperboreans, and the Ethiopians. A "supernatural storm" drives Odysseus beyond the human realm, and he wanders in limbo. He sees many cities and learns the minds of many beings, none of which conforms to the Greek model of civilization in every respect.[47]

The same logic of the frontier, Michèle Rosellini and Suzanne Saïd have shown, structures Herodotus's accounts of the customs of foreigners on the fringes of the Greek world.[48] The more remote a people, the more uncivilized it is, as indicated by progressively more promiscuous sexual behavior or by the shift from eating grain to eating animal flesh and then to controlled and finally uncontrolled cannibalism. Suprahuman peoples inhabit the frontier as well: the long-lived Ethiopians, for example, despise bread as if it were manure and are nourished on milk and boiled meat, which, they say, the earth gives spontaneously. The mythic and ethnographic accounts differ, not in the way they contrast foreign with Greek, but in their attitude toward the material. The poet uses it to entertain, while the historian, judging from Herodotus's qualifying "they say" concerning the Ethiopians, maintains some distance.

According to Diodorus, Amazons share the frontier with the gorgons and the Atlantians.[49] He gives no details of the gorgons' appearance but does identify them with the gorgon slain by Perseus; they must be monsters who belong to the bestial realm. The Atlantians are "the most civilized [*hēmeros:* literally, "tame"] of the peoples in those parts," and among them the gods are said to have been born. They rise above the human estate to nearness with the gods, which constitutes a paradisiacal state. The presence of Amazons in remote areas says nothing about their whereabouts other than that they are not in Greece. It is, rather, a spatial expression of their reversal of patriarchal culture: Amazons blur the categories that classify the domains of male and female. But we can go still further in emptying their homelands of any specifically Amazon content.

Diodorus claimed, and modern scholars have reiterated without hesitation, that the Libyan Amazons did not practice agriculture. The context of his remark is an ethnographical description of the peoples of Libya and of the Amazons' home island. There is no doubt that it is another instance of reversal and frontier logic.

> The [Amazon] women, the mythographers say, lived on an island called Hespera [i.e., Evening], from its position toward the setting sun. The island was in the marsh Tritonis. . . . It was of good size and was filled with fruit-bearing trees of every sort, from which the inhabitants took sustenance. It also had a multitude of flocks of goats and sheep, whose milk and meat their owners ate. The nation did not use grain at all, because its use had not yet been invented.[50]

Agriculture in Greek gender roles, as we have seen, separated men from women in an alimentary code. Food production is an activity of men. By attributing it to Amazons, Strabo signifies their usurpation of the male role in this area as well as in war. Agriculture also separates men from the animals and gods; it is a human activity. Its presence serves to define a culture as human— that is, civilized by the Greek norm. Its absence is a mark of bestiality or divinity. Hesiod's men of the golden age are near-divine, a race reflecting pure justice; they are supported by the earth's spontaneous bounty. Men, who know injustice as well as justice, must toil upon the earth for their food. The Cyclops Polyphemus, whose mind is lawless, is ignorant of agriculture. He labors at herding sheep that eat the spontaneous bounty of his country, while across the bay is an island where goats flourish of their own accord.[51] The men of the golden age are above human culture; the Cyclops is below it. Neither has agriculture. By denying Amazons agriculture, Diodorus is saying nothing about their way of life. He means that they do not belong to civilization. Moreover, the fact that their island provides them with food without toil aligns them with figures whose mythic status is not in doubt.

Agriculture produces grain, the tame (hēmeros) food of civilized (hēmeros) men. Opposed to it are the raw food of animals, including their own flesh, and the ambrosia (am- [not] + bros- [mortal]) food of the gods. Before the discovery of grain, men lived like beasts. Nothing useful for life had been discovered—houses, fire, or tame food. According to Moschion, a tragic poet of the third century B.C.,

> there was once that age when humans had a mode of life like the beasts and dwelled in mountain caves and sunless ravines. For there was not yet the roofed house or wide city fortified by stone towers. The black glebe, nurse of grain, was not cut by curved plows, nor was the worker, the iron pruning hook, tending to the flourishing gardens of Bacchus's wine. But the earth was barren, holding silent, and flowing with water. Food of eaten flesh gave them a way of life by killing one another.[52]

Diodorus brings the same correlation of tame food and civilized men into his account of the Libyan peoples. He describes three tribes: one practices agriculture, another herding, and a third that "leads a bestial life."

> They [the third tribe] remain in the open air and pursue savagery [*to agrion*] in their customs. They have no part of tame [*hēmeros*] food or clothing but cover their bodies with goatskins. Their leaders have no cities. . . .[53]

Agriculture and herding are activities of the Greeks, so the first peoples are said to lead a life "not completely savage or differing from human civilization [literally, "tameness"]." The third group consumes no grain; it is savage. The Amazons' lack of grain and wine (the islanders drink milk) puts them in a precivilized state, one simultaneously bestial and godlike.

The sources, then, are not describing Amazons from research or even from free invention. The latter is perhaps most surprising to those critics for whom the opposition of real/not real or historical/not historical is inseparable from the Amazon myth. The mythographers' statements belong to an ethnographical code that goes back to Homer. Amazons, it says, are from the twilight zone of animal/human, god/human, and male/female beings; they are not civilized.

Long before the Persian wars Amazons were located in Asia. Persians and Ionian Greeks lived in Asia, and after the wars the Athenians developed conceits about both which contributed to the myth. The repulse of the barbarians proved to the Athenians the superiority of free men over slaves. Among the slaves they included the Ionians for failing to press their revolt in the early 490s and thus for betraying their preference for servitude.[54] One explanation offered by the writer of the Hippocratic treatise *Airs, Waters, Places* (fifth century B.C.) was that slaves had no motive to study war or to risk everything by being brave since the rewards of victory went to the master. He also gives another, less objective reason:

> Concerning the lack of spirit and cowardice of the inhabitants—the fact that the Asiatics are less warlike and are tamer [*hēmeros*] than the Europeans in their character—the seasons are especially responsible. They make no great changes either to heat or cold but are nearly the same. For there are no shocks of the mind nor strong shifts of the body. From such conditions the temper is likely to be made wild [*agrios*] and to be imparted with a headstrong and passionate spirit more than when things are always the same. For changes are what stir up the mind of men and do not let them be at rest. For these reasons it seems to me the Asiatic race is without strength.[55]

The very land that nourishes them predestines Asiatics to be spiritless and tame. Aristotle, in the *Politics*, provides a more elaborate scheme of the notion. In his model, Greece is a median between the extremes of Europe and Asia:

> Nations in cold climates and those in Europe are full of spirit but impoverished in intellect and skill. Therefore they continue for the most part to be free but lacking in political organization and ability to rule over their neighbors. The nations in Asia are intelligent and skilled of mind but are spiritless. Therefore they continue to be ruled and enslaved. The race

of the Greeks, just as it occupies the middle area geographically, shares in both. It is spirited and intelligent, and therefore it continues to be free and of the best organization politically. It is capable of ruling all peoples should it gain a unified constitution.[56]

The following oppositions distinguishing Greece from Asia emerge from these texts:

Greece	Asia
changes in weather	no changes in weather
spirit	no spirit
warlike	cowardly
wild	tame
free	enslaved

Homologous with these is the opposition hard/soft. "Soft men," says Herodotus, "are wont to spring from soft lands." In this he concurs with the Hippocratic writer:

You will find generally that the physiques and characters of men are of a piece with the nature of their land. When the land is fat, soft, and well-watered, and the water is close to the surface so that it is hot in summer and cold in winter, and the seasons are favorable, there men are generally fleshy and without visible joints, moist, ill-disposed to suffering, and cowardly in spirit.[57]

A fragment of Ephorus preserved by a Byzantine grammarian proves that such "geographical predestination" was applied to the Amazons.[58] The reference to the "mixture of the place" identifies Ephorus's source with medical theory; health in Hippocratic medicine consisted of the proper mixture of blood, phlegm, yellow bile, and black bile. The fragment also provides crucial evidence for reversal: if men are soft, women are hard.

They say concerning them [Amazons] that they excelled over the nature of men, giving as the reason the mixture of the place, that it was wont to give birth to female bodies

stronger and bigger than male bodies. I consider it natural
that the constitution of all is the same so that the reason is
senseless.

Asiatics are soft because they are born and raised on a soft land.
Its softness, conversely, makes the women bigger and stronger, a
polarization that conjures up the Amazon. To be soft in Greek
thinking, whether biological, musical, or utopian, is to be unmanly,
hence, womanly, the antithesis of the male warrior. Aristotle, in
speaking of both humans and larger quadrupeds, pronounced female nature "softer, more quickly domesticated, more submissive
to the hand, and more ready to learn." Soft harmonies are forbid-
den Plato's warriors. "We pursue philosophy," Pericles said in his
encomium to Athens, "without softness."[59]

Agrios denotes "savage" and *hēmeros* "civilized," in the code of
homelands or agriculture, but in the military code expressed by
Herodotus, the Hippocratic writer, and Aristotle, *hēmeros* denotes
"tame" or "passive," and *agrios* "spirited." The juxtaposition of
codes discloses the duality of these terms and the values they
designate. Savage spirits are antithetical to civilization as animal is
to human; yet animal spirits make warriors strong, and strong warriors are vital to the continuance of civilization and of the city and
of the way of life synonymous with both. Civilized tameness differs from unmanly tameness in degree only. They are distinguish-
able only when polarized. To affix differences between them
somewhere along the continuum is the problem. One too easily
misjudges the median. In one direction excess of animal spirits carries with it the loss of civilization in savagery. In the other direction, tameness to an excess breeds cowardice and invites invasion
and enslavement. Alvin W. Gouldner, in *Enter Plato,* has under-
lined how pervasive the threat of slavery was in the ancient world:

> Greek culture insisted that to be successful is not to be im-
> mune to the worst disaster. Even the highest were vulnerable,
> not simply to the ordinary setbacks of life, but to what
> Greek values define as the very worst thing that could befall
> a man; for, indeed, by Solon's time slavery was commonly

felt to be even worse than death, and, to understate it for the moment, the Greeks had a particular dislike of death.[60]

Loss of freedom, forced submission to the will of another, is the suppressed anxiety of Pericles' proud claim. The curiosity that is to become philosophy arises first among Ionians, who are despised for their cowardice and servitude. Athenians, Pericles insists, are different. Despite their festivals, games, and relaxed way of living, so unlike that of their enemies, they are ready to face all dangers with courage.[61]

In the language of the Amazons' homelands Asia has three meanings. It is a land outside Greece on the frontier of civilization and savagery. Through the assimilation of Persians to Amazons it is a land that is soft, one that emasculates its men and virilifies its women. It is a land of slaves. These themes, in the air in postwar Athens, were exploited by Aeschylus for a crucial scene in the *Agamemnon*.[62] After ten years in Asia, Agamemnon returns to greet his wife before the door of his house. He has been too long there; he has become soft, an oriental despot whose shoes are "slaves" for his feet. In the "battle" for control of the doors, Agamemnon is overcome by a woman.

Geographical predestination obviated the need to distinguish civilized from unmanly tameness by polarizing them through meteorological, political, and medical codes. The assimilation of Persians to Amazons achieves the same effect through combat. Soft Persian men evoked in the imagination hard (Amazon) women. The Greeks defeated the Persians, who would have enslaved them as they had the redoubtable Amazons. The link connecting Persians, Amazons, and the meaning of their homeland in Asia is slavery.

What the myth says of Amazon customs and homelands derives neither from inquiry nor from independent creation. It is a product of the Greek view of the human condition as civilized, mortal, Greek, and, most of all, male. When men cease to be men, the world ceases to be ordered; and the topsy-turvy world of the Amazon results.

CHAPTER 4

Amazons: Sons and Daughters in Limbo

THE LIFE OF every Greek was governed by a twofold imperative: that boys become warriors and girls become wives and  mothers. In practice it was a single imperative, since the state's need for soldiers was urgent, and the social structure held out only reclusion or prostitution as alternatives to motherhood. Greek society focused on the adult male warrior. The ability to bear arms, to join with others, defined citizenship. Changes in the constitution at Athens widened participation in political life by expanding the base of fighters, but it did not alter the emphasis on the adult male fighter.

This emphasis meant that girls, women, boys—even men too old to fight—were outsiders. As fringe elements, they emerge in mythology as figures antithetical to the ideal. Their situations are conceptually opposed to those of the adult male warrior. They are at once characters in stories about what happens when things go awry and elements in a system of codes used to conceptualize and support, however unconsciously, the nature of the warrior and, concomitantly, the nature of marriage. Because such figures collectively occupy the same position vis-à-vis the ideal, they are nearer to one another in imagination than in appearance or reality.

RITES OF TRANSITION

This chapter approaches the Amazon myth from the viewpoint of the rites of transition that every youth had to undergo to become a full member of society. With characteristic insight, Jean-Pierre Vernant has described the transition of boys and girls from social infancy to adulthood:

> [I]f the rites of passage mean for the boys access to the warrior state, for the girls associated with them in these same rites and often themselves submitted to a period of seclusion, the initiatory tests have the value of a preparation for conjugal union. On this level . . . are revealed the bond and, at the very same time, the polarity between the two types of institutions. Marriage is for the girl what war is for the boy: for both, they mark the fulfillment of their respective natures, the moment when each departs from a state in which each still shares characteristics with the other. Thus a girl who refuses marriage, renouncing at the same time her "womanness," is in some way cast back toward war to become paradoxically equivalent to a warrior. On the level of myth this is what we see in female figures of the type of the Amazons and, on the religious plane, in goddesses like Athena: their warrior status is linked to their condition as *parthenos* [virgin], each having made an eternal vow of virginity.[1]

What Vernant means when he remarks that a girl who fails to make the transition becomes "paradoxically equivalent to a warrior" is clear, and the paradox vanishes if we keep in mind that girls and boys are polarized identicals. The one may collapse into the other because both are made identical by their opposition to the adult male fighter.

The Amazon myth concerns the specter of daughters who refuse their destiny and fail to make the accepted transition through marriage to wife and motherhood. Amazons are daughters in limbo, neither men nor women nor nubile girls. They hate men and vie with them in hunting and war. In combat they surpass all but the hero. They are beautiful women who arouse men sexually, but their erotic appeal cannot be civilized in marriage, its proper sphere, and so is loose, socially unproductive, and dangerous. Like Greek girls, Amazons mate with males and bear children, but they do not leave their mothers for the house of a husband, nor do they become, like Greek women, wives and mothers of sons. They are mothers of daughters who live with mothers. Such relationships, while describing the Amazons' liminality, conceal the structure by which they are organized. The Amazon myth, though it deals with daughters and, as we shall see, sons in limbo, is about the warrior and marriage.

Amazon customs reverse a polarity whose ideal is the adult male. Society is essentially concerned with his functions as hoplite soldier and progenitor of hoplites. Successful transition from childhood results in warriors or mothers. Failure to make that passage evokes monsters of the imagination, figures created by antithesis to the values accorded the adult male as hoplite and father. Such are the Amazons, for they reverse the hoplite on two planes —war and marriage.[2]

Transition rites, as outlined by the anthropologist Edmund Leach, are ceremonies that proclaim and effect passage from one social status across social boundaries to another.[3] Such rites include those attending on birth, naming, puberty, marriage, and burial, as well as initiations into closed societies and religious mysteries; all are found among the ancient Greeks. The emphasis here is on puberty rites, which, it must be understood, prepare for the social as well as the physical maturation of the child.

Transition rites are remarkably similar the world over. In Leach's synthesis they fall generally into three stages: rites of separation, rites of marginality, and rites of aggregation. Rites of separation remove the initiates from their present condition and time reference. Once separated, the initiates exist in limbo, a state of marginality where they are without social status and are outside ordinary time and space. The final stage involves rites that are intended to reintegrate them into society and time in a new status.

The present analysis begins with the sacrifice to the Amazons offered on the seventh of the month of Pyanepsion, the day before the festival of Theseus.[4] It was probably not an ancient sacrifice but rather an existing rite that was taken over when Cimon nationalized the family cult of the Phytalidae. Pisistratus had already linked two of the month's festivals to Theseus: the Oschophoria and the Pyanepsia were explained by the hero's Cretan adventure.[5] The festival of Theseus was conducted by descendants of families whose members sailed to Crete with Theseus. On the seventh day of the month sacrifices were also offered to Theseus's teacher as well as to his helmsman on the Cretan voyage.[6] Another sacrifice, such as the one to the Amazons, would appear to be nothing special. But all of these rites are connected with Theseus's youth, while the sacrifice to the Amazons belongs to his maturity. What, then, made the sacrifice appropriate?

One reason comes to mind immediately: Cimon wanted to join his father's defense of Athens at Marathon (and his own policy of ridding the eastern Aegean of Persians) with a precedent from the city's formative past. Bringing in the Amazons whenever possible had propagandistic value, but more was needed than a general's whim to expand the sacred calendar.

The Attic month of Pyanepsion comprised the lunar cycle beginning in late October at the outset of the Greek autumn. It was a season for plowing and sowing and for harvesting the grapes.[7] It was also a time of renewal, of reinvigorating the land for the new planting, celebrating the new wine, and welcoming new members into the family. During Pyanepsion, boys became citizens, brides were enrolled with their husbands' ancestral brotherhood (phratry), and women were confirmed as mothers. Pervading the festivals of the month were the male/female opposition and motifs of transition rites. The Amazons fit in well because they are organized that way themselves.

Oschophoria

The Oschophoria, "Carrying of the Oschae," celebrated on the sixth of Pyanepsion, was a festival for the ripe grape. It was named for a procession from Dionysus's sanctuary in Athens to the Temple of Athena Skiras at Phaleron, the city's original harbor on the Saronic Gulf. Leading the procession were two young boys or striplings who were dressed as women and carried vine branches with grape clusters on them, the *oschae*. A race to Phaleron was held among epehebes (eighteen-to-twenty-year-old males) from each tribe. During the sacrifice and banquet that followed the procession and race, the celebrants told one another stories. The festival ended in a revelry back to Athens amid mixed cries of joy and grief.[8]

Transition motifs and sexual polarity are evident in the race and procession. Competition was a lifelong activity of men and a regular part of the ephebe's training for adulthood. The masculine runners are opposed to the feminized boys by "striving furiously" against one another; the boys walk at a ceremonial pace. Transvestism often characterized transition rites; it denoted a marginal state preceding the rigid conformity of adult sexual roles. The mixed cries, half-joyous and half-sorrowful, reflect the changes of harvest and coming of age, the changes of death and rebirth.

Theseus had to be on the minds of those who attended the banquets, and his myths were undoubtedly often told. Perhaps the Amazon episode was among them. That would account for the presence of an Amazon grave stele just inside the Itonian gate, the gate on the southeastern side of the city leading in from Phaleron. The revelers, walking by a monument whose purpose had long been forgotten, may have attributed it to an Amazon.[9]

Apaturia

The Apaturia was from earliest times a festival of the phratry which lasted three days and was an affair for admitting new members into the brotherhood.[10] The occasion was as much social as religious, and sacrifice to the gods of the family and phratry attended each admission. The third day of the Apaturia was the *Koureōtis*, a name derived from a root combining the "cutting" of the hair and "young man." It refers to the cutting of the youth's hair, which was allowed to grow long during his childhood. The act was a symbolic mutilation of the kind common in transitions. The boy's infancy was cut away and dedicated to Artemis, the Cherisher of Children. He was now a *kouros,* a clipped one, a young man. On this day also the boy was presented by his father to the phratry for acceptance. As the father had done soon after the child's birth, he and his witnesses now swore that the candidate was his son and had been born of a solemnly married woman.[11] Entry into the phratry was not automatic, and not to be accepted was to be deemed a bastard and to lose not only one's rights of citizenship but one's father or son. During the fifth century B.C. the deme came to share this function with the phratry; transition rites for young men at physical puberty continued to be held in the phratry, while those for social puberty (at the age of eighteen) were taken over by the deme.

Thesmophoria

In counterpoise to the masculine festivals was the Thesmophoria, an ancient fertility rite administered exclusively by citizen-women.[12] Its rituals, dedicated to Demeter and Kore, were celebrated all over Greece, but they were kept secret and so are little known. On the first day of the festival, the eleventh of the month, the women left their houses and families and convened in a sacred area, where they set up huts. No men were present. On the next day they dressed in mourning clothes and fasted while sitting on branches of a nauseous-smelling plant. On the thirteenth they changed into brightly embroidered robes and celebrated the Calligenia, the feast of "Fair Offspring." The name probably refers to Demeter as goddess of fair offspring and to Kore/Persephone as fair offspring.

Sexual polarity is visible in the women's withdrawal from their husbands and in their observance of ritual purity in the form of abstinence from sexual intercourse. The branches on which they sat were from the *agnus,* the "pure" or "chaste" plant, which was considered an antaphrodisiac. Its stench contrasted with the perfumes of erotic attraction, as did the ritual title of the women, Melissae (bees). That insect was known for its abhorrence of perfumes and sexual intercourse. At one point during the Thesmophoria women brought up from chasms the decayed remains of pigs and the remnants of dough serpents and phalli. These had been sacrificed during the summer "in token of the birth of the fruits and human beings." The darkness of the caverns, the serpents that were said to dwell therein, the unsavory remains, and the gloom over the festival contrast with the feasting and competitions of the masculine festivals, which were held outdoors or in a well-lighted, festive house of the phratry.

The emphasis of the Thesmophoria is upon the fertility both of the earth and its avatars, the women. The women withdrew not simply from their everyday routines but from the human realm in order to enter into a participation with the goddesses. They likened their fasting and sitting on the ground to events in Demeter's loss and recovery of her child. Yet more is involved than the reenactment of a myth. Demeter and Kore/Persephone are archetypal for the mother who gives birth to a daughter who bears a daughter, the chain sustaining human existence. Through the mystery of Demeter, women are confirmed as bearers of life; they experience themselves as one with the goddess and her grain. C. G. Jung's insights are relevant here:

> Demeter and Kore, mother and daughter, extend the feminine consciousness both upwards and downwards. They add an "older and younger," "stronger and weaker" dimension to it and widen out the narrowly limited conscious mind bound in space and time, giving intimations of a greater and more comprehensive personality which has a share in the eternal course of things. . . . We could therefore say that every mother contains her daughter in herself and every daughter her mother, and that every woman extends backwards into her mother and forwards into her daughter. This participation and intermingling give rise to that peculiar uncertainty as regards *time:* a woman lives earlier as a mother, later as a

daughter. The conscious experience of these ties produces the feeling that her life is spread out over generations—the first step towards the immediate experience and conviction of being outside time, which brings with it a feeling of *immortality*. The individual's life is elevated into a type, indeed it becomes the archetype of woman's fate in general. This leads to a restoration or *apocatastasis* of the lives of her ancestors, who now, through the bridge of the momentary individual, pass down into the generations of the future. An experience of this kind gives the individual a place and a meaning in the life of the generations, so that all unnecessary obstacles are cleared out of the way of the life-stream that is to flow through her. At the same time the individual is rescued from her isolation and restored to wholeness [Jung's italics].[13]

Psychological interpretations tantalize the desire for understanding, and every reconstruction of a mystery remains speculative. Yet Jung's views are consistent with the sexual polarity of the Thesmophoria. It was a time for mothers of daughters, a bond that excludes the male and imperils his order. Should the mother overvalue that bond, as does Aeschylus's Clytemnestra, undervaluation of her ties with her son and husband would ensue. The passion of Demeter and Persephone is that of a mother forcefully separated from her daughter. The daughter who stays with her mother and who has the force to resist the male is the Amazon.

The festivals of Pyanepsion display sexual polarity and motifs of transition, and even though they have no bearing on the Amazon myth itself, they do help reveal the Amazon as a figure created by the failure of girls to make the transition to adulthood by marriage and the failure of boys to make that transition by military training.

BOYS IN TRANSITION

At eighteen years of age young men entered a period of marginality consisting primarily of military training and separation from their families. This was the second step toward full citizenship, the first being registration on the citizens' roll of their deme. The practice was a natural outgrowth of the universal military service imposed on all male citizens. It was apparently so standard that the ancients took it for granted; the sources pass over it in near silence until the last part of the fourth century B.C. Scholars now agree that it long antedates its codification by law as a two-year program (c. 335 B.C.).[14]

For the first year the ephebes were stationed on guard duty near the harbor at Piraeus. They were trained in the use of weapons and participated in religious festivals across Attica. At the end of the year they were paraded before the community and given a shield and spear. At this time they also swore an oath of citizenship in the shrine of Aglaurus on the Acropolis. A likely occasion for the oath would be the festivals of return during Pyanepsion. It is probably no coincidence that the families of Salaminian immigrants who administered the Oschophoria also furnished priestesses to the cult of Aglaurus.[15] In the second year of their training the ephebes were barracked apart in forts on the frontier and "went around the country" as a lightly armed defense force. During their period of service they wore black robes and were exempt from most legal obligations. Afterward, "they were with the others" as full citizens.

This program undoubtedly expanded and regularized existing practices designed to use training in arms and civic indoctrination as a rite of transition to membership among the citizen-soldiery. Ephebes were separated from their infant surroundings, dressed in robes of black to signify the latency of their social status, and assigned to the frontier. Positioned on the fringe, they "went around," an expression that recalls their official name, *peripoloi* (goers around). When the borders were still being contested, they probably sought out enemies. When they did fight, the inadequacy of their weapons before hoplite armor forced them to rely on trickery and ambush.

In a pioneering study, Pierre Vidal-Naquet has discovered in the ephebe's marginal state elements that predate and oppose that of the hoplite.[16] He examines the Athenian program by comparing it with the Spartan and Cretan forms, which were less institutionalized and therefore are a guide to earlier Athenian practices. The ephebe is an antihoplite, Vidal-Naquet has shown, in that he carries light weapons as opposed to the panoply carried by the hoplite. Unlike the latter, the ephebe does not fight in formation. He fights on the borders, along and with metics (noncitizens) rather than beside citizens, for the city's fertile fields. He fights by ruse and at night; his mythic model is Melanthius (Blacky), who kills Xanthus (Blondy) by means of trickery. The hoplite, on the other hand, fights in daylight, when there is no chance for deception.

The hunt is another activity of the border regions in which the ephebe stands in opposition to the adult male. The latter pursues game in a way that reinforces the ethic of the hoplite; he hunts by day, without dogs or nets, armed with a pike, and in the company of others. The hunt of the young man is the antithesis: by night, nets and dogs, solitude, trickery. Figures like Hippolytus, Melanion, Adonis, and Atalanta, who flee marriage for the hunt, are examples of the ephebe gone awry; that is, they embody or are created by the concept of the ephebe who remains in limbo and refuses to grow up. We will return to them because they are cognate with the Amazons: all are creatures begotten by extrapolating the variables in limbo between social infant and hoplite, virgin and married woman.

GIRLS IN TRANSITION

Marriage was the rite of transition undergone by most Athenian girls. A few from aristocratic families carried "unspoken things" in the festival of Athena or "did the bear" for Artemis of Munichia or Brauron. Of the latter festival it is said that all girls between five and ten years of age had to dress in long yellow robes and imitate a bear walking on its hind legs as a prerequisite for future marriage. Thus would they rid themselves, according to Aelianus, of all savagery.[17] The transition from savage to civilized state would have been most evident in the shedding of their robes, which they did at one point in the ceremony.[18]

The typical wedding ceremony took place over three days.[19] On the first day the bride, who could be as young as fourteen, bid farewell to her childhood by dedicating her toys to Artemis. An anonymous poem from the *Greek Anthology* records the moment in one girl's life:

> Timareta before her wedding dedicated her drums, her lovely ball, hairnet, and dolls to Artemis of the Lake, a virgin to a virgin as is fitting. To Artemis also did she dedicate her virgin's dress.[20]

On this day or a few days before, the bride's father dedicated her to the gods of marriage—Hera, Zeus, Artemis, and the Moirae (Fates). He ended the sacrifice by cutting a lock of the girl's hair and offering it to Artemis. This act, similar to the clipping of the ephebe's hair, marks another coincidence of the sexes in transition.

Another motif of transition is the nuptial bath taken by bride and groom. Water for the bath was brought from Callirrhoë, a spring on the Ilissos not far from the Itonian gate and its Amazon stele. A boy or girl, garlanded with myrtle, carried the water in a specially shaped vessel amid a procession of kinswomen bearing torches. Myrtle was regarded as an erotic plant, and in vase paintings of the scene Eros is shown hovering above the procession. The nuptial bath washed away the old self while the procession publicized the wedding.

On the second day the gate and walls of the house were strewn with myrtle. The bride's father sacrificed to the gods of marriage and feted the groom, his family, and friends. During the festivities the bride was led in by her attendants. She was veiled, in a state that appears to have signified her latency from the society around her. At the end of the feast she uncovered her face and was seen among men for the first time. Her unmarried state was now over, its loss perhaps compensated by the gifts of "the unveiling" presented to her by her husband. By now it was dark, and the

journey to the husband's house was made under the light of
torches. The wedding couple mounted the chariot waiting at the
door and was driven away by a friend of the husband. A procession
followed. The couple was met by the husband's parents, who
showered the bride with dates, dried figs, and nuts, surely a fertility
rite. Husband and wife then entered the bridal chamber, at whose
door the husband's friend stood guard.

The ceremony was completed the next day, the first of the
bride's life in her husband's house. Gifts arrived from her family to
mark the occasion. Her reproductive capacity and labor were now
owed to her husband's family. Marriage within Attica did not
necessarily mean a great distance between the girl and her mother,
but women did not as a rule brave the hazards of travel. Plutarch
advises the bride to transfer her affections to her husband's parents. Sophocles gave this lament to Procne in his lost *Tereus:*

> Now I am all alone. I have often thought about the nature of
> women—how we are nothing. As young girls in our father's
> house we live the sweetest life. Children are always nursed by
> pleasant ignorance. When we come to maturity and under-
> stand, we are pushed off, sold off, away from ancestral gods
> and parents. Some go to strangers, others to foreigners, some
> to congenial houses, others to houses full of bickering. This
> lot, whenever one night puts us under its yoke, we must be
> contented with and praise.[21]

Though both sexes must successfully pass to adulthood, society
focuses on the male. For that reason, the successful transition for
the girl is not so much that she becomes wife and mother as that
her husband be made father. This viewpoint accounts for Euphiletus's treatment of his new wife. On trial for killing his wife's lover
after having caught him *in flagrante delicto,* Euphiletus says:

> When I thought it best to marry, fellow Athenians, I brought
> a wife into my house. For some time I arranged things so
> as not to bother her or let her do whatever she wished too
> much. I kept watch on her as far as was possible and attended

to her as was reasonable. But when a child was born to me, I
began from then to trust her and gave over to her everything of myself, considering this to be the greatest relationship.[22]

Not everything a defendant says need be believed, but Euphiletus
expected his behavior to be approved by the jurors.

The girl is aggregated into society as an adult not by marriage
but by making her husband a father. A reason for this, suggested
by comparative studies with modern Greece, is that her marriage
with a strange or near-strange man of almost twice her age did not
culminate a relationship established in courting but rather initiated
one. A baby sealed their partnership if not their love.[23] That is
why, in the structure outlined here, the goal of the boy's rite of
transition is to become not only a warrior but a father.

THE COMPOSITION OF THE AMAZON

The Amazon is made of elements taken from the transitional
boy and girl and is liminal between social infancy and the adult
male as warrior and father. On the one hand, the Amazon is like
the girl, once dedicated to Artemis, who refuses to carry through
the marriage ceremony and enters upon the boy's adult role. What
for the boy constitutes aggregation is for the girl liminality made
of reversals. For society the outcome is no future hoplites because
by using her reproductivity for herself the Amazon denies it to
society. But the Amazon is also like the boy who, sent out to the
frontier to hunt and defend the borders, never returns for marriage and a place in the hoplite formation. There would then be no
hoplites of the present or future because there would be no
fathers. The Amazon's reproductivity is denied to society in this
case by her flight from it.

The girl who refuses her destiny (motherhood) can in Greek
antithetical thought only be an *antianeira,* a female opposed to
(*anti-*) and compared with (*anti-*) a man (*aneir-*).[24] Thus, by virtue

of her marginal position with respect to the adult male, she is imagined as a female hunter (Atalanta, Artemis, Nicaea) or warrior (Amazon). The boy who refuses his destiny is a male imagined, similarly by virtue of his marginality, as hermitic (Melanion), non-sexual (Hippolytus), hypersexual (Adonis), or as feminized. The fourth variation is connected to the myth through its religious code. The feminized male is likened to worshipers of Eastern deities such as Cybele and Artemis of Ephesus, deities whose devotees were wild women and eunuchs. Amazons, the myths have it, worship these gods, which is to say that they worship gods who emasculate men. The Amazon, then, is one permutation of a structure behind a part of Greek mythology. Unique to her is the combination female, militant, fighting against men, sexual attraction, dominance in marriage. Moreover, since the last are included in the first two, the Amazon is unique for being a warrior who is a woman.

Herodotus's account of the Amazon and Scythian youths provides a link between the reversals discussed in the previous chapter and the structure defined here. His account is based on the motif of reversals of patriarchal customs. Moreover, the very scene of the action he describes puts the conceptual structure into literal spatial terms. The boy or girl, it must be remembered, spent his or her infancy in the same society into which, after the rite of passage, he or she was aggregated. So the movement is one of *out* and *back,* whether accomplished literally or ritually.

The Scythian youths go out of the society of their fathers' houses, where they were "the youngest." They enter the limbo of the Amazon, a place between the Thermodon, irretrievably lost because of the Amazons' ignorance of sailing, and the houses of the Scythian fathers. Like the Amazons, the youths engage in hunting and plundering, using horses and weapons consistent with horses, the bow and javelin. They engage in the ruse of pursuit and retreat. The Amazons show their liminality by fighting and by controlling sex and marriage. Once the Scythians have mates, they wish to be aggregated into society, but they cannot go back: Amazons are creatures of the margin who suspend their mates in limbo with them.

AMAZONS LIKE UNTO MEN

The reversals considered earlier have established the Amazons' liminality as resemblance to men in war and control of marriage. That resemblance is the substance of Hellanicus's description of their army: "golden-shielded, silver-axed, female, man-loving, male-infant-slaying." Gold and silver are soft metals unsuitable for weapons, but as precious metals they symbolize here, as they do on Achilles' shield in *Iliad* 18, the suprahuman prowess of those who wield such weapons. Amazons are sexual, not virginal, and they desire men while rejecting male babies; thus is a concise summary of their control of a nonpatriarchal marriage system written.

This same liminality is expressed differently in the myth of the Amazon Penthesilea. The episode was narrated by Arctinus (eighth century B.C.?) in the epic *Aethiopis,* which is known from an epitome by the Neoplatonist Proclus (fifth century A.D.): [25]

> The Amazon Penthesilea arrives to aid the Trojans in war.
> She is the daughter of Ares and a Thracian by birth. Achilles
> kills her while she is fighting at her best, and the Trojans
> bury her. Achilles kills Thersites, who railed at him and re-
> proached him for loving Penthesilea.

Though this myth appears on black- and red-figure vases of the classical period, it is found only in postclassical literature. Quintus Smyrnaeus's (fourth century A.D.) treatment of it is elaborate but faithful to the essential element: Penthesilea inspires love in Achilles *after* her death. Quintus describes her arrival at Troy and her death repose as follows:

> As when Dawn comes down from weariless Olympus with the
> lovely-haired Seasons, glorying in her shining steeds, amid
> all is she conspicuous, so beautiful is she though the others
> are blameless, thus did Penthesilea come to Troy preeminent
> among the Amazons. The Trojans rush from all sides and
> wonder greatly when they see the high-greaved daughter of

weariless Ares alike to the blessed immortals. The beauty of
her face was awesome and radiant. Her smile was lovely, and
beneath her brows her eyes, sparkling like rays, aroused desire. Modesty blushed her cheeks, and over them was a godlike
grace clothed in war prowess.

Though she lay fallen in dirt and gore, beneath her lovely
eyebrows shone her beautiful face, even in death. The Argives,
crowding about, were amazed when they saw her: she seemed
like the blessed immortals. She lay on the ground in her armor like tireless Artemis, daughter of Zeus, sleeping when
weary from chasing swift lions in the lofty mountains. Aphrodite, beautiful garlanded wife of mighty Ares, made Penthesilea radiant even in death to cause the son of blameless Peleus
to grieve. Many men prayed that when they came home they
would sleep in the bed of a wife like her. Achilles suffered
greatly in his heart, that he slew her and did not bring her to
Phthia as his shining wife, since in height and beauty she was
blameless and like the immortals.[26]

Quintus compares Penthesilea to Dawn: both stand out from
among their companions. The simile goes back to the *Odyssey:*

> White-armed Nausicaä led off the singing and dancing for
> them. As arrow-spreading Artemis goes along the mountains,
> very lofty Taygetus or Erymanthus, delighting in boars and
> swift deer, and with her sport nymphs, daughters of aegis-
> bearing Zeus, who roam the wild, and Leto is glad in her
> heart, for above all tower the head and brows of Artemis, and
> she is easily known, though all are beautiful; thus did the
> unwed virgin Nausicaä stand out among her handmaidens.[27]

Nausicaä has come to the river to wash clothes. Athena appeared
the night before in a dream gently upbraiding her for leaving them
soiled when marriage was near. She would need clean ones for herself and her escort. When she asks her father for a wagon and
mules, Nausicaä omits mention of marriage: "she was ashamed to
speak to her father of her lively [or lusty] marriage."

Quintus undoubtedly knew the simile; Nausicaä's eagerness for marriage and her modesty are meant as counterpoint to Penthesilea. Nausicaä will soon meet Odysseus, whom she would marry; Penthesilea will soon encounter Achilles, who kills her and then would marry. But Penthesilea is compared to Dawn. Why Dawn? A reason may be prolepsis for the death of her son, Memnon, later in the poem. But poets, even second-rate ones like Quintus, are not simple. Dawn was notorious for her sexual aggressiveness; she did not play the female's waiting game. She "became impassioned and raped" Tithonus, Cephalus, Orion, and Clitus.[28] Rape elsewhere is an activity of men, the sexual equivalent of war, where the phallus becomes a sword to humble and dominate. As the Amazon assumes the male role in war, so Dawn assumes it in rape. Dawn complements the Amazon's liminality. Behind both figures is that of Nausicaä, eager for marriage.

Penthesilea's eyes are said to arouse desire and to sparkle. Quintus surely has in mind Homer's description of Aphrodite's breasts as arousing desire and her eyes as sparkling. He uses the same words as Homer. In Greek physiology love and beauty were thought to emanate or breathe forth from the eyes. Penthesilea radiates sensuality, which the Trojans receive through their eyes: they wonder when they see her. Yet modesty or shame, the feeling that inhibits natural desires, reddens her cheeks. It is the attribute of the perpetually unwed virgin, Hestia, over whom the shameless goddess of sexual desires has no power.[29]

The grace (charis) upon Penthesilea is clad in war strength. Grace is the charm of beauty that attracts men and urges them to accept a gift—originally, the gift of the woman herself. In the Iliad, Iphidamas paid much for his bride's charis but died before he knew it. Charis belongs to Aphrodite; its avatars are the Graces; her companions, who execute Zeus's orders to Aphrodite to pour charis over Pandora. War strength, on the other hand, is instilled by Ares and has nothing to do with Aphrodite, as Zeus reminds his daughter: "The works of war have not been given to you, my child. You have concern for the arousing works of marriage. Leave these other things to swift Ares and Athena."[30] Penthesilea is a freak, a hybrid monster composed of elements discrete in the normal worlds of gods and men. She is a Hestia radiant with Aphrodite, and Aphrodite clad in Ares. She is an Amazon: unwed, seductive, sexual, militant.

Penthesilea's death repose expresses liminality in terms of gods. The purpose of marriage is to beget and socialize children; for that end, and not for their own pleasure, does erotic attraction bring the sexes together. Too little eroticism discourages union; too much encourages sexual indulgence.[31] The goddess of virginity, Artemis, and the goddess of license, Aphrodite, represent the polar extremes of eroticism in marriage. The Amazons share masculine pursuits with Artemis but not her virginity. Like Aphrodite, they charm men but do not share her willingness to become wife and mother for them. They have no place in marriage. Their eroticism, present in Penthesilea's lovely eyebrows and beautiful face, is dangerous outside marriage and is therefore put beyond harm. The Argives long for a wife like Penthesilea, and Achilles wants her as his wife, only *after she is dead.*

Amazons are the daughters of Ares and the nymph Harmonia. The latter was originally a cult title of Aphrodite at Thebes, but we cannot see in that title Aphrodite as their parent.[32] The attribution to Harmonia was made by writers at Athens, among them Pherecydes, who had no idea of the name's provenance. Even so, Aphrodite is connected with Ares in cult by her worship as a war goddess, and in literature, beginning with Homer. In the *Iliad* she helps him when he is struck unconscious by Athena, and in the *Odyssey* she is caught in bed with him by her husband, Hephaestus.[33]

Aphrodite and Ares are the opposites, love and war. He is war as murderous fury and savage bloodthirstiness, while she is eroticism outside marriage or against marriage as well as in marriage. She is patron of courtesans; she cheats on her husband without shame and inspires Helen to leave her husband for Paris. These gods—Ares unequivocally and Aphrodite at times—represent war and sexual desire as destructive forces.[34] Thus they constitute a divine code for the liminality of the Amazon in marriage and war.

Finally, liminality as "likeness unto men" is seen as armed hostility toward marriage. According to Ephorus, the Amazons, raped by their husbands, kill them and do not welcome back other men who have left for a war. Another version has the Amazons originating from women whose husbands are slain treacherously. They take up arms, avenge their mates, and then slay all the remaining men lest any woman be more fortunate than the rest. Ephorus tells a similar tale in explaining the origin of the Sauromatians, whom the Greeks regarded as descendants of Amazons.[35]

In the *Theseis* an armed Antiope, put aside by Theseus in favor of a Greek wife, Phaedra, attacks the wedding party and is slain by Heracles. In a later version she is killed by the wedding guests. Plutarch labeled the story fiction and invention.[36] It is probably modeled on Pirithous's wedding feast, an original episode of the Theseus myth, at which the Centaurs, becoming inebriated, try to rape the bride as she is being escorted into the room and are killed by the bridegroom and Theseus.[37] Amazons and Centaurs are found together in the battles of the Athenian treasury at Delphi, the murals of the Theseum, the sculptures of the Temple of Hephaestus, and the metopes of the Parthenon. Page du Bois has suggested rightly that both represent extremes of the Greek male. The all-female Amazons, like the all-male Centaurs, are antithetical to the ideal.[38] Du Bois has also shown that the Centaurs embody the negation of marriage in that they are descended from a breach of marriage. When Hera reported that Ixion had tried to rape her, Zeus fashioned an image of her from clouds and put it in bed with Ixion. Ixion impregnated it with Centaurus, who later became the father of the Centaurs by mating with mares. At the wedding feast the Centaurs attack the marriage bond at its crux—the exchange of women by men. The two episodes clearly have the same meaning: an assault on marriage from without, one by lust (Centaurs), the other by weapons (Amazons).

AMAZONS OPPOSED TO MEN

The Amazons' likeness to men defines them in the Greek mentality as rivals of men; that is, they are viewed as opposed or antithetical to the male as father. This antithesis takes the form of their refusal to grant men their reproductivity. Again, all Amazons refuse patriarchal marriage and restrictions on sex. On the one hand, they do so actively by usurping men's roles and using their reproductivity for their own purposes. On the other, they remain extrapolations of the boy who refuses to grow up, and their threat is passive: they run away. Figures representing this plane of the myth's structure flee patriarchal society and its marriage for the wilds and the life of the hunter. Melanion, Adonis, and Atalanta are cognate with the Amazons; Nicaea and, despite his sex, Hippolytus are Amazon hunters.

The youth Melanion hates women and flees marriage for the life of the solitary hunter:

> There was a young man, Melanion, who in flight from marriage went into the wilderness and lived in the mountains.
> He hunted the hare with woven nets and kept dogs. Never again did he return home, because of his hatred, so much did he loathe women.[39]

Adonis is the issue of an incestuous union of daughter and father. He is very beautiful and even as a boy inspires Persephone and Aphrodite with desire. True to his birth, he is a seducer and a hunter of easy prey, deer and hares. He dies, gored by a boar.[40] Atalanta, abandoned as an infant by a father who would have a son, is nursed by a bear and reared by hunters. When she grows up, she guards her virginity and remains ever-armed. She kills two Centaurs who try to rape her, participates in the hunt for the Calydonian boar, and defeats Achilles' father, Peleus, in wrestling. According to Theognis,

> Iasius's daughter, though ripe to wed, refused men's marriage and fled. Drawing tight the war-girdle, blonde Atalanta tried

to accomplish the unaccomplishable [or accomplished useless things] by leaving her father's house. She went into the high peaks of the mountains, fleeing arousing marriage, gift of golden Aphrodite. In the end she came to know it despite her refusal.

Forced into marrying, Atalanta sets up a courting race. Armed with weapons, she pursues her naked suitor. If she catches him, he dies; if not, she marries him. Many die until Melanion, a different Melanion from the hermit, challenges her. As he runs, he drops golden apples given to him by Aphrodite. Atalanta stops to pick them up and loses the race. Later they make love in a grove sacred to Zeus and are changed into lions, an animal thought never to mate with its own kind but with leopards.[41]

These myths have been treated by Pierre Vidal-Naquet and Marcel Detienne with richness and sensitivity.[42] Their analyses support the present view of Melanion, Adonis, and Atalanta as liminal figures and cognates of the Amazon. Flight from society, variously imagined as misogyny, hypersexuality, and/or the life of a hunter, characterizes each. Motifs of the ephebe are present in Melanion's methods of hunting, Adonis's sexuality outside marriage, and Atalanta's wrestling and racing.

There are no Amazon hunters during the classical period. Little can be made of Nicaea in Nonnos's (fifth century A.D.?) epic poem on Dionysus's adventures. She is too late and she lacks the foundation in the classical and earlier periods which Quintus Smyrnaeus's Penthesilea enjoys. Briefly, the shepherd Hymnus falls in love with Nicaea, who flees the marriage he offers. His attentions become a nuisance, and she kills him. He is avenged by Dionysus, who gets Nicaea drunk and rapes her in her sleep.[43] For classical times this aspect of the Amazon myth appears as Hippolytus, son of Theseus and an Amazon.

Hippolytus, like his father, belonged originally to Troizen, across the Saronic Gulf. Troizenian girls dedicated a lock of their hair to him at their weddings and sang songs about his death. His myth probably was invented there to explain his cult and it passed into

Athenian lore through the aggrandizement of Theseus in the late sixth century B.C. In outline his myth is as follows: Phaedra becomes impassioned for her stepson, Hippolytus, but is rebuffed by the chaste hunter. She lies to her husband, claiming Hippolytus tried to rape her. Theseus prays to his father, Poseidon, to destroy Hippolytus. The god responds, and Hippolytus is killed. Phaedra commits suicide, and Theseus is left alone.[44] The myth was popular in the fifth century, particularly on the tragic stage, being treated in two plays by Euripides and one by Sophocles. The extant play by Euripides, his second, which contrasts Hippolytus's devotion to Artemis with his withdrawal from Aphrodite, was produced in 428 B.C. The dates of the others are unknown.

Hippolytus is a liminal figure between virginity and marriage. He dies in limbo, a virgin killed for his virginity. For that reason girls at Troizen who were about to die ritually as virgins sacrificed to him their hair and mourned his death. He embodies in the way of a Greek divinity a reality of nature—the suffering and sorrow of adulthood.[45] In mourning him the maidens mourn the death of their maidenhood, while, through the hero's intercession, they are inspired to see that loss as part of "the nature of things" and so find relief and consolation. A temple of Aphrodite stood in Hippolytus's shrine in both Troizen and Athens, a sign perhaps of the fact that, unlike Hippolytus, the girls are reborn as sexual adults.

Hippolytus is a myth, a figment of the failure to mature. Compared to the father defined by the Amazon myth's structure, he is socially useless: his power to reproduce does not contribute sons to the family or state. What better image of his condition than Euripides' sexless human wandering the wilds with an immortal virgin who shuns men and is invisible even to a favorite?[46] His eroticism, on the other hand, operating in the extant play as the passion aroused in the married woman Phaedra, is outside marriage and thus open for Aphrodite to use destructively. She—that is, Hippolytus's erotic appeal—destroys Theseus's marriage as well as Phaedra, Theseus, and Hippolytus himself.

AMAZON RELIGION

Amazons worship Ares and the Phrygian Mother, Cybele, under that name and as Artemis of Ephesus and Thracian Artemis Tauropolos. Since these were historical cults, some see in the Amazons' religion evidence for their existence.[47] In terms of the myth, however, the worship of Ares, as well as his parentage of the Amazons, may be explained as a religious code for their militancy. Cybele and both Artemises were deities of fertility, the wild, and wild beasts. Their rites were orgiastic, attended by frenzied dancing and music; their votaries were women and eunuchs. They were regarded by the Greeks as foreign and barbaric, while castration was a practice identified with Asiatics, the soft men, and was considered revolting.[48]

A clue to the meaning of Amazon worship is provided by Philostratus (third century A.D.) in his life of the philosopher Apollonius (first century A.D.). Apollonius is upbraiding the Athenians for their conduct at a festival of Dionysus:

> A woman captain from Caria sailed with Xerxes against
> you, and there was nothing womanly about her. She had a
> man's dress and weapons. You are softer than the women of
> Xerxes' day. You dress in a manner that insults yourselves,
> O young men, old men, and ephebes. The ephebes of old went
> to the shrine of Agraulus and swore to die for the father-
> land and to bear arms. Now probably they will swear to revel
> in a Bacchic frenzy for the fatherland and to take up the
> thyrsus. They do not carry helmets but in women-aping form,
> in Euripides' phrase, cut a disgraceful appearance.[49]

Dionysus, though entering the Amazon myth late, was identified with Cybele from her introduction into Greece in the fifth century B.C. Their rites were similar in purpose, achieving through music and dance an ecstasy culminating in union with the god. Dionysus was a womanish deity, and his worshipers were primarily women; despite his divinity he was held to be cowardly.[50] Apollonius cast the opposite of the ephebe as a feminized reveler of Dionysus who carries the god's sacred wand, the thyrsus, instead of a helmet. A parallel from the classical period is the young Pentheus of Euripides' *Bacchae* (probably 405 B.C.), who fails to overcome Dionysus by force of arms and is turned by the god into a devotee, a reversal emblematized by dressing him in women's clothes. [51]

The religion of the Amazons is an expression of their nature as *antianeira:* they worship gods who foster war and the castration of men. In this their religion complements male rape. Men rape and sexually kill Amazons. Amazons, through their religion, castrate and sexually kill men.

·CHAPTER 5·

Amazons
and Androgyny

THE WEAK POINT of Greek patriarchy is its dependence upon women for sons. Beginning with Hesiod, literature and myth attest  to men's longing for another way. "O Zeus," laments Euripides' Hippolytus, "if you wanted to sow human seed, you ought not to have provided the means from women." Hippolytus would buy sons from the gods. A common fantasy was male parthenogenesis. Zeus expropriates the woman's part, giving birth to Athena from his head and to Dionysus from his thigh. His triumph is complete when his wife, Hera, resenting his audacity ("How dare you give birth to gleaming-eyed Athena alone?"), can do no better by herself than to produce the monstrous Typhaon, who resembles neither gods nor men, or, in another version, the lowly and crippled Hephaestus. But it remains for Aeschylus's Apollo to pronounce the "scientific" basis for denying parenthood to the mother:

> The mother is not the parent of the thing called a child but a nurse of a newly sown seed. The one who mounts is the parent. She, like a host for a guest, protects the young plant, for those a god harms not.[1]

Amazons have no such weakness. They bear their daughters for themselves, reducing dependence upon the opposite sex to the minimum. Amazons are figments of the threshold between social infancy and adulthood, but they are as well on the *limen* between male and female. They share in the strengths of both sexes and so are stronger than either. Mightier than ordinary men, they challenge even the hero, limited as he is by a single-sexed nature. They are hybrids, androgynous monsters, neither male nor female.

Androgyny was familiar to the Greeks as a condition of oriental deities, whose power it expressed in biological terms. Bisexual gods manifested fertility and the life cycle and were recognizably foreign. The Greeks, who were given to single-sexed gods, reacted to them in various ways. The Aphrodite of Cyprus, bearded and having male genitals, was worshiped in the masculine form of the name, Aphroditos. Cybele/Agdistis they rendered single-sexed; Dionysus, who had to be accepted, was feminized. Androgyny crept into Hesiod's *Theogony* (a work influenced by oriental myths) as parthenogenesis and disappeared with the rule of Zeus and patriarchal marriage.[2] The androgynous god, made up of elements drawn from sexuality, fertility, and the cycle of life and death, was perceived as fearful and strange. It is therefore not surprising that fear of the Amazons, as well as their formidability as foes, is attributed to their androgyny. This explains, moreover, why through death in combat or death by rape they are reduced in the myths to either nubile girls or mothers.

THE DEATH OF AN AMAZON ANDROGYNE

The first heroes to kill Amazons are Achilles, Bellerophon, and Heracles. The first of these has been discussed. Bellerophon's combat with the Amazons has no sexual overtones and is simply part of Iobates' attempt to kill him.[3] Bellerophon goes to Proetus, king of Argos, to be purified from pollution for an accidental murder.

Stheneboea, Proetus's wife, falls in love with him and tries to seduce him. Rebuffed, she lies to her husband, claiming that Bellerophon made advances to her. Proetus becomes enraged with jealousy and sends Bellerophon to the king of Lycia, Iobates, with instructions that Bellerophon be killed. Iobates orders Bellerophon to fight the Chaemera, the Solymi, and the Amazons, expecting each time that he will be killed. But he slays them all, as well as the warriors of the king who were chosen to ambush him. Iobates, awed by Bellerophon's strength, gives him his daughter in marriage and later his kingdom.

The Amazons here are merely female warriors; they balance the male Solymi and the animal Chaemera. Bellerophon defeats every manner of opponent—fierce men, fierce women, and a fierce animal. The Amazons are women but are more warrior than woman. The remaining possibility for Bellerophon to surpass—namely, the gods—comes in his final deed, his attempt to scale Olympus on Pegasus. What finally routs him, in fact, is neither fierce nor warlike. Lycian women raise their skirts and display their genitals to him, and he runs in fright from the gorgon.[4] The motif is that of the Perseus myth, which will be discussed at length later in this chapter.

Heracles' quest for the girdle of the Amazon queen is told in the following way by Apollodorus in *The Library:*

> Hippolyte had the girdle of Ares as a mark of her excellence in fighting. For this girdle Heracles was sent because Eurystheus's daughter, Admete, wanted it very much. Taking volunteer allies in one ship he set sail. . . . He put in at the harbor of Themiscyra. Hippolyte came to him and asked why he had come and promised to give him her girdle. Hera, likening herself to one of the Amazons, went among the throng, saying that the strangers were carrying off the queen. The Amazons rushed on horseback to the ship with their weapons. Heracles, realizing that this was happening by deceit, killed Hippolyte and took the girdle. He then fought the rest and sailed away to Troy.[5]

The focus of the myth is the girdle, which causes a critical problem. Is it a warrior's belt for securing his tunic and armor or is it a woman's girdle? The myth describes it as Ares' token of prowess in war. Why, then, does a pampered princess want it? How can one belt have such different qualities—the strength to gird armor, the elegance to grace a woman's waist? The contradiction vanishes when we see the girdle as not a girdle but a homologue for the Amazon's liminality. Heracles triumphs over the male side of the androgyne by killing the Amazon warrior. His triumph over the female side is latent and depends upon the synonymity of *zōstēr,* the word used for Hippolyte's girdle, and the common word for the woman's girdle, *zonē.* For a woman to loosen her *zonē* for a man was both a prelude to and a metaphor for her sexual submission.[6] When Heracles takes the *zōstēr* by force, he symbolically rapes Hippolyte. Rape, the violent use of the male genitalia, becomes the means to humiliate and aggregate the Amazon's female aspect. It becomes explicit with Theseus, Athenian hero and rapist *par excellence.*

Two versions of Theseus's acquisition of an Amazon wife are told:

> According to Philochorus and others, Theseus sailed to the
> Black Sea as part of Heracles' expedition against the Amazons
> and received Antiope as a prize. But the majority of author-
> ities, including Pherecydes, Hellanicus, and Herodorus, say
> that he sailed with his own force later than Heracles and that
> he took the Amazon as a captive of his spear.[7]

The influence of the Ninth Labor is evident, but the rape of the Amazon belongs to Theseus alone. In the older tradition he was credited by the mythmakers with raping Helen and Ariadne, and in the new myths of the Pisistratid period, with raping the daughters of Cercyon and Sinis. The rape of the Amazon belongs among the latter, although most likely the Helen myth was its model.[8] In the Helen myth Theseus and Pirithous, as sons of gods (Poseidon and Zeus, respectively), deem it their due to marry daughters of Zeus. They abduct Helen from Sparta and take her to Aphidna in Attica. Since she is too young to marry—Apollodorus says that she is twelve to Theseus's fifty years—they leave her with Theseus's mother, Aethra, while they go to the underworld to carry off its queen, Persephone. Meanwhile, Helen's brothers, Castor and Pollux, invade Attica and rescue their sister. The key similarities between the old and new myths are the common exploits of Theseus and Pirithous and the invasion that results from the rape.

Visual representations of the myth, popular on vases between 510 and 490 B.C., appear to have been modeled on the nuptial chariot ride.[9] Like the groom, Theseus drives the bride from her house to his. Pirithous corresponds to the groom's friend who stands sentry outside the chamber on the wedding night. Later tradition had Phaedra as Theseus's wife and the Amazon as a concubine. Nuptial motifs from vases contemporary with the myth's genesis, however, support the suggestion made above, that the Amazon was Theseus's wife in the *Theseis*.

The sexual element, now in the open, is put into the context of marriage. Theseus does not simply rape the Amazon; he aggregates her by force into the role prescribed for Greek women, thereby killing her as an Amazon. Whereas Heracles killed and "raped" Hippolyte, Theseus rapes and "kills" Antiope, for that is her name in the *Theseis*. According to the epic, Antiope fights against him only after he puts her away in favor of Phaedra. As long as Theseus respects the marriage, a commitment secured by the birth of a son, she stays a wife.[10]

If the reconstruction proposed in Chapter One for the Amazon episode in the *Theseis* is correct, then Antiope fights beside Theseus against her fellow Amazons. Another version says that she falls fighting for Athens.[11] She is no ordinary wife; she "works" with her husband in a common enterprise as an equal. By restricting women to the house, Athenian men deprived themselves of their wives' contributions in the public sphere.[12] Marriage with a whole person and equal partner was unthinkable, but the strength and creativity of such a union slips out nonetheless as the couple's defense of their city.

Achilles kills Penthesilea—to discover someone he would marry. Heracles kills Hippolyte, and the girl who would be man is stripped of her illusions. Theseus rapes Antiope, socializing the virginity derived from the transitional boy. The masculine side of the Amazon androgyne is cut away, and the feminine side is ravished into submission. The daughter must marry.

CLYTEMNESTRA AS ANDROGYNE

Whatever ideas are explored through the Amazon myth, the essential motif remains the daughter in marginality. Treatment of the Amazon as an androgyne is also governed by this motif. Amazon androgyny does not, therefore, carry the full message of androgyny in Athenian mythmaking. The daughter is the woman in only one capacity; there remain the more formidable aspects of wife and mother. To understand the Amazon myth fully, the purview of the inquiry must be widened to include Aeschylus's Clytemnestra as androgyne.

Like the fearful androgynous god, Clytemnestra is composed of elements deriving from sexuality, fertility, and the cycle of life and death. In the scene before she murders Agamemnon, Cassandra prepares us to see her as beyond the human:

> What should I call this hateful thing whose sting is death? A serpent or Scylla dwelling in the rocks, bane to sailors? A raging Mother of Hades breathing an implacable curse against her kin?[13]

Clytemnestra entangles Agamemnon in a bathtub with a great robe and strikes him three times with a sword. She kills as an androgyne with the weapons of both sexes. The audience has just heard his cries, "I am struck," coming from within the house and seen the Chorus of elders shatter into bewildered individuals, milling around with fruitless activity, vivid theater for the breakdown of the social order on the death of the king. Then Clytemnestra appears at the door, vaunting over her victim:

I did it. I will not deny it, in a way that left no flight or
defense. An endless net, like one for fish, I threw around him
—a direful wealth of robe. I struck him twice. With two
groans he went slack at the knees. When he is fallen, I give
him a third blow, votive thanks for Zeus-beneath-the-earth,
savior of corpses. He fell and shot forth his life.[14]

Clytemnestra usurps the male weapon, Aegisthus's sword, which,
like his manhood, is at her bidding: "He lights the fire at my
hearth."[15] Before wielding it, she confines Agamemnon in a bathtub and ensnares him in a robe. Women, usually slaves, bathed the
men. Andromache's servants heated water for her husband on the
day Hector no longer would come home.[16] After a long separation
a bath given by the wife would be a natural prelude to intimacies.
Cassandra suggests such a consummation (Clytemnestra will
"wash" [or gladden] her bedmate with bath waters) even as she
foretells another: Clytemnestra will catch her husband, a fish in a
net.[17]

The robe is a product of women's hands, perhaps even Clytemnestra's. Many hours were spent weaving, a vital and prominent
contribution of women to the wealth of the household. Aeschylus
says nothing of the robe's provenance, but the vision of Clytemnestra weaving at home an endless net for Agamemnon, as her sister
Helen was weaving one at Troy for so many others, accords with
his view of her.[18] Moreover, the robe is "a direful wealth," a metaphor that points to another of the wife's tasks.

Women had the responsibility of guarding their husband's store-
room and property inside the house. Clytemnestra misleads her
husband's herald by calling herself the "watchdog of the house,
good to him, hostile to his enemies." On the surface the words
evoke Odysseus's description of the ideal married pair, and even
their usual application as the prescription for the ideal warrior
does not jar.[19] But Clytemnestra is no watchdog. She is, as Cassandra sees, "a hateful bitch," and her words do not hide her true
intent from those who understand: "a bitch in the house, hostile

to him on behalf of his enemies.''[20] Sword and weaving, tokens of
separate domains in the Greek order of things, are united to destroy
Agamemnon. Such a union happened once before, in the so-called
"tapestry" scene at the door of the house.[21]

Agamemnon enters from the east, stage right. He is still mounted
in his chariot. Cassandra is beside him. She is about to die, "a
relish" on Clytemnestra's vengeance and a scapegoat for all the
golden girls bedded by him at Troy.[22] Agamemnon, lavishly
dressed, is surrounded by his entourage of attendants and soldiers.
Clytemnestra emerges from the doors of the palace. Several servants follow; they carry brownish-red tapestries. The principals
avoid speaking to each other. He addresses the gods; she, the Argive
elders. Agamemnon speaks of his victory and his friend Odysseus,
reminders of Iphigenia.[23] He promises to take counsel before the
full assembly of citizens. Then, with a prayer that past victory ever
attend, he moves to leave the chariot and enter his house. Clytemnestra blocks him, relating the anguish of a woman left home with
rumors of her husband's death. She excuses Orestes' absence, a
hidden reminder of the other absent child, Iphigenia, but she barely
keeps him from being obvious about her obsession with nets and
the death of the man before her. When she does turn to Agamemnon, it is with hyperbolic praise and a request:

> My sufferings are behind me, all endured, and with heart free
> of grief I hail this man, watchdog of our stables, saving cable
> of the ship, tall pillar of the lofty roof, only son of the father,
> land seen by sailors against their expectations, sweetest day
> to see after a storm, spring water for a thirsty traveler. Pleas-
> ant it is to escape all necessity. I deem him worthy of this
> greeting. Let there be no envy present. We have borne much
> adversity in the past. Now for me, dear heart, step forth from
> this chariot, but do not put your foot on the ground, O lord,
> destroyer of Ilium. Servants, why do you hesitate, you who
> were ordered to strew the ground of his path with tapestries?
> Let his way become spread with crimson this instant, so

justice may guide him into *a house he never expected to see* [italics added]. As for the rest, wisdom not subdued by sleep will set in just order with god's help whatever is fated.[24]

Agamemnon begins to reply: "daughter of Leda, guardian of my house," and with the word "guardian," Clytemnestra knows she has him. He disclaims such honors as befitting gods, not mortals, knowing they are dangerous just as he knew that the sacrifice of his daughter was "a heavy doom" of pollution. The tapestries meanwhile are being spread before him. He protests against treading the crimson way, but does so weakly and in pieties hollowed by lust for glory, betraying the same passion he showed at Aulis. Clytemnestra has re-created the moment when he killed her daughter. Robes spreading before him reify the Chorus's vision of the folds of Iphigenia's dress falling around him as she was lifted over the altar.[25] Whereas the daughter's voice was checked by the mute violence of gags, her mother fawns on him with a tongue, Cassandra says, he knows not:[26]

> *Clytemnestra.* What, do you suppose, Priam would do if he did what you did?
> *Agamemnon.* Walk on the tapestries. No doubt.
> *Clytemnestra.* Please, do not feel shame before the censure of men.
> *Agamemnon.* Yet the talk shouted by the people carries strength.
> *Clytemnestra.* The man free of envy is the man without anything to envy.
> *Agamemnon.* To desire battle is not womanly.
> *Clytemnestra.* For the blessed to be overcome is fitting.
> *Agamemnon.* Do you really think the victory worth the struggle?
> *Clytemnestra.* Be persuaded. You have the power. Yield to me willingly.[27]
> *Agamemnon.* Very well, if you think it best, let someone remove quickly my shoes, slaves for my feet to tread upon.[28]

All eyes in the theater are riveted on Agamemnon as a slave kneels to loosen his sandals in a vision of oriental obsequiousness. He has been too long in soft Asia. Clytemnestra has grown hard; she defeats him in battle for the door and makes ready the way into the house as "he never expected to see" it. This is the meaning behind the words quoted in italics above.[29]

Persuasion and desire for battle, themselves opposing male values, are united by the androgynous Clytemnestra. Agamemnon enters the house as she would have him enter it—squandering the wealth of costly tapestries. The treading or kicking of untouchable things is established in the trilogy as a motif for the corruption brought on by excessive wealth and the impiety it induces.[30] That imagery connects the treading of the tapestries with the impiety at Aulis, where, despite "the sheep abounding in the fleecy flocks," Agamemnon sacrificed his daughter, Clytemnestra's "most beloved pain."[31] The blood that polluted his hands fell to the ground, and blood, in the *Oresteia*, "congeals and washes not away."

> There is a law that drops of blood, once flowed to the ground, other blood alone recalls. For murder shouts for an avenging Erinys bringing from those perished before a second ruin on ruin.[32]

It is Iphigenia's blood Agamemnon now treads, calling it forth from the ground with his own blood.

Clytemnestra is victorious over Agamemnon because he is hers to kill. She fails to persuade Cassandra, who is Apollo's victim. But when she gives up in disgust at Cassandra's recalcitrance, she says something revealing: "I have no time to rub this doorway." This is an obscenity for preparing the genitals for sexual intercourse.[33] Foul language is not easily admitted into tragedy, and despite the unanimous reading of the manuscripts, the Greek is usually changed to give "at this door" or "outside." Yet Aeschylus, according to Quintilian, could be uncouth as well as sublime.[34] Later Clytemnestra reviles the dead Cassandra as prophet and sexual partner in a crescendo that culminates in a crudity from the docks: "Here lies his [Agamemnon's] faithful consort, speaker of prophecies and stroker of his erection on the ship's benches."[35] Scholars have changed the manuscripts there, too, but men utter such words, and Aeschylus is mimicking the scurrilous cant of sailors. His Clytemnestra knows it the way that she knows the aftermath of a fallen city: she talks "like a man." What the first obscenity reveals is her perception of a woman's body as a house and the entering of it as penetration. That explains why she speaks of her bedmate, Aegisthus, as kindling the fire at her hearth. The house and hearth symbolized, as we have seen, the inner space of the female.[36] In that vein the Chorus addresses Aegisthus as "woman, you stay-at-home waiting for those returning from battle, shaming the bed of a man."[37] But Clytemnestra is not one to wait passively for the man to come in. Her persuasion at the door is turned into seduction by her perception of the house as woman. She is aware of Agamemnon's phallus, as the image of the "tall pillar" suggests. As he walks across the tapestries, she says:

> There is the sea. Who will dry it up? It nourishes the juice,
> good as silver and ever-renewed, of purple dye for clothes.
> The *house* with gods' help, o Lord, possesses it for the having.
> The *house* knows not how to be poor. I would vow the
> treading of many tapestries if it had been enjoined upon the
> *house* in oracles and myself managing payment for your
> life. For while the root exists, leafage comes to the *house* and
> extends shade against the scorching dogstar. Now that you
> have come to the hearth of the *house,* warmth signals its
> coming in winter, and when Zeus makes wine from bitter
> green grapes, then there is coolness in the *house,* since the
> man in authority frequents the *house.* Zeus, Zeus Accom-
> plisher, accomplish my prayers. May you attend to whatever
> you intend to accomplish [italics added].[38]

Agamemnon is the root; the tree that grows to protect the house is Orestes. The man is the generative force that sustains the house, and Orestes is his seed.[39] It is not "the man in authority" Clytemnestra is talking about, although that is what Agamemnon hears, but "the full-grown," sexually mature, man. (*Anēr teleios* allows both meanings, as well as a third, "an unblemished man"; see note 27.) He can warm her house when he comes to its hearth, a sexual reference comparable to her description of Aegisthus. *Epistrōphōmenou* (translated above as "frequents") means "haunting, visiting, going in and out of," and has no sexual connotation by itself. After Cassandra uses the simple form of the verb, *strōphōmenon,* to refer to Aegisthus's frequenting Agamemnon's bed, one cannot be denied.[40] Besides, "house" is too often on Clytemnestra's lips to be only idle repetition. Agamemnon warms her hearth as he goes in and out of her house: her language conjures the movements of the sex act. Persuasion becomes seduction; entering becomes penetration, then copulation; and murder within the house becomes castration.

Finally, Clytemnestra's prayers are fulfilled in the pleasure of a death that is an androgynous climax.[41] She continues with her description of Agamemnon's death:

> Breathing out a spurting slaughter of bloody gore, he hits me with a dark shower of bloody dew. In it I pleasure no less than the new-sown field in the joy sent by Zeus at the birthing of the buds.[42]

All would recognize the reference to the sacred marriage of Earth and Sky, a fertility symbol:

> Holy Sky passionately longs to penetrate Earth. Passion grips Earth to achieve union. Rain from her bedfellow, Sky, falls and impregnates Earth. She gives birth from men to the pasturage of the flocks and the grain of Demeter. The fruit of the trees ripens from the moist joy. And I, Aphrodite, am responsible for this.[43]

Agamemnon's dew is equivalent to the Zeus-sent joy and Sky's moist joy. Their rain/semen quickens Earth to life; Agamemnon's blood/semen delights "the Mother of Hades."[44] Imagery of fertility is inverted to become that of death. Zeus and Sky are above Earth; Agamemnon is within Clytemnestra. When he shoots forth his life over her, she experiences it as his semen being ejaculated within her. Male and female orgasms are united in an androgynous climax that negates Aphrodite's creative passion and the fundamental distinction of human existence and cosmic order.

THE DEATH OF CLYTEMNESTRA AS ANDROGYNE

Clytemnestra rules as matriach over a house and a city characterized by reversals of the patriarchy. In the tapestry scene she welcomes Agamemnon into her domain by a reversal: she makes of him a woman. Clytemnestra seizes the male sphere, however, without relinquishing the female. She keeps control of the household wealth and sacrificial rites. Seduction at the door, suggested by the imagery, may have come out in the staging; she is not one to eschew eroticism to win. She offers her breast to Orestes in a stunning appeal for life, a breast whose maternal function has been denied by the nurse, Cilissa, in the previous scene. Only the erotic remains.[45] Clytemnestra conquers as androgyne with the persuasion of male words and female sex and kills with the violence of the sword and entangling web. Her androgyny makes order impossible since it confounds the distinction most essential to it—that between male and female. The androgyne must be slain.

The Daring Woman

Aeschylus gives two indications of the meaning of Clytemnestra's death; both are in the *Libation Bearers*. The first comes at the center of the play, and so of the trilogy, in a choral ode that is complex in language and allusion. The text is corrupt, and the translation an approximation.

> Many dreadful pains of fears the earth nourishes. The clutches
> of hostile monsters abound on the sea for men. Lights
> raised on high in midair do harm, and winged creatures and
> those walking on earth. You could tell of the windy wrath
> of storms.

But who could speak of the excessively daring temper of a man and all-daring loves of women rash at heart, consorting with the ruins of men? The female-dominating loveless love conquers and corrupts the conjugal unions of beasts and men.

Let him know who is not flighty in thoughts and learn of the forethought the woman, the child-destroying, headstrong, fire-burning daughter of Thestius devised: she kindled the murderous brand of her child that was his coeval from his birth cries, coextensive in life to his death day.

There was in legends another bloody Scylla to hate, who destroyed her husband for an enemy's sake, persuaded by Cretan necklaces of wearied gold, the bribes of Minos. Shamelessly with premeditation, she robbed Nisus of his immortal hair in his sleep. Hermes caught up with her.

Since I am recalling pain that cannot be soothed, here is a hateful marriage, abominable to the house, and schemes devised by a woman's mind against a man bearing arms, an awesome and bitter thing against her husband for his enemies' sake. I honor the hearth not heated by passion, an undaring spirit in women.

The tale of the Lemnian women is first in the narrative of evils. It is an abomination loathed by peoples everywhere. A man takes the Lemnian woes as a standard of the dreadful. Their race of mortals perishes, dishonored by a pollution detested by the gods. No one respects what the gods hate. Which of these do I include unjustly?[46]

The Chorus sings of women infamous for crimes against men. Althaea threw into the fire the brand that held her son's life. Scylla killed her father for jewelry. The women of Lemnos killed their husbands and fathers. In their company the Chorus enrolls Clytemnestra, her deed henceforth part of the catalog of infamies preserved in myths.

The Chorus decries "the excessively daring temper of a man and the all-daring loves of women rash at heart." "A man" may refer to Agamemnon or be a generalization. In any case, the Chorus's emphasis is on "the female-dominating loveless love [that] conquers and corrupts conjugal unions of beasts and men." *Thēlykratēs* (female-dominating) is ambiguous; it would normally mean "dominating the female," but the context requires "female love of dominance." The women of the ode, spurred by a passion that leads to bold action, subdue men. Their victory gives no true victory; it corrupts because victory is won by the sword of men.[47] The theme fits Clytemnestra fully; she kills her husband and she has a hot hearth and a woman's bold spirit. Cassandra says of her: "She dares such things: the female is the murderer of the male." These words immediately precede her speculations on Clytemnestra's nature (quoted above, page 93). Orestes also speculates about Clytemnestra:

> She who devised this abomination against the husband from
> whom she bore the weight of children beneath her girdle,
> once loved, now, as it appears, a hated evil—what does she
> seem to me? a sea monster or viper whose nature putrefies by
> touch without biting: such is her boldness and unrighteous
> mind.[48]

The same complex of themes occurs in Cassandra's prophecy of Agamemnon's death,[49] in her speculations and those of Orestes, and in the ode: conjugal love, monsters, boldness, death of the male. What does it mean? The women described are all impassioned for power or dominance. They dare to act against the male and marriage. The mother kills the son, the daughter the father, the wife the husband. Marriage is the institution that tames and civilizes female bestiality. Once it is broken down, women outside its control revert to their bestial nature. They become the animals they once were.

Theirs are deeds heinous in outcome, but to confuse outcome with daring is to be hoodwinked by Aeschylus's mythmaking. They are deeds censured speciously for their result but actually because they are done by a woman on her own initiative. Daring is a quality admirable only in men. Although it is no more than the capacity to act on one's will in order to achieve goals, daring is what it means to be a person—that is, manly. Thucydides reports a speech of the Syracusan Hermocrates encouraging his men to face the Athenians. It highlights the maleness of daring.

> For daring men such as the Athenians, those who are daring in return would seem the most difficult to handle. The Syracusans could equally confront the Athenians with the very daring used by them to attack and terrify neighbors often not much weaker than themselves. Hermocrates said that he knew well that the Syracusans, by daring to resist the fleet of the Athenians against their expectations, would come out ahead. . . .[50]

Even in excess, as in Agamemnon's sacrifice of his daughter, daring is ultimately forgivable in a man. In the last plays Agamemnon becomes the beloved father cruelly slain and Athena's partner in leveling Troy. This is so because daring is manliness of strength and spirit, qualities on which the city or household depended for its survival. For that reason the man of daring was valued, whatever his failings in other virtues.[51]

In a woman, on the other hand, daring is despicable. Greek mythmaking envisioned only a single end: Innate female bestiality, unleashed from Cecrops's marriage, turns against the male in acts of aggression. The polar outlook of the Greeks allowed no alternative. Daring is a condition of mind that strives for dominance and victory, so the daring woman must strive for victory. And, since women in marriage are "in order"—that is, tamed, civilized, defeated—the only victory to be won is over men. Daring expressed by a woman, even a woman with the best intentions, comes out badly for the male, since the woman has annulled marriage as the foundation of male order.

Deianira, in Sophocles' *Women of Trachis* (early 420's B.C.?), ventures to influence things outside the house; she tries to turn her husband, Heracles, away from the younger woman Iole and back to herself with a robe dipped in what she believes is an aphrodisiac. She seeks to restore Heracles to her bed as her husband. Her preparations complete, she hesitates before the Chorus:

> I cannot fathom or understand daring, bad women. I loathe
> women who have acted daringly. If somehow I can surpass
> this young thing with my love spells and charms on Heracles,
> the deed is done, unless I seem to be acting rashly. If so, I
> will stop. [52]

Deianira knows her act is daring and assuages her misgivings with hopes of success. But she plans badly. She kills her husband and destroys his house with poison she mistook for a love charm. There could be no other end. Heracles renews the house by marrying his son to Iole, but Deianira, in trying to save it, unwittingly becomes a Clytemnestra.

Clytemnestra, Deianira, and the daring women of the ode stand for the same thing: the woman who would be her own person. They do so negatively because such a woman is outside the Athenian patriarchy's definition of woman and marriage as a structure of order between the sexes.

The Perseus Myth

The second indication of the meaning of Clytemnestra's death comes when the Chorus of Trojan slave women conceptualizes Orestes' last encounter with her in terms of Perseus's beheading of Medusa. They are encouraging him not to shrink from his awful task:

> Be bold when your time to act comes. Cry back at her
> screams of "Child" with a louder scream, "a Father's Child."
> Then accomplish blameless vengeance. Hold in your breast
> a Perseus's heart for kinsmen beneath the earth. For those
> above exact vengeance. They will be grateful. Make bloody
> destruction of that baneful gorgon within. Look at the culprit
> and kill him. [53]

Aeschylus had already presented his trilogy on the Perseus myth by the time of the *Oresteia*. The titles—*Drawers of the Net, Daughters of Phorcus,* and *Polydectes*—designate the major episodes of the myth; how Aeschylus handled them is little known. But the analogy with Perseus is important, and so the myth must be examined in some detail. The paraphrase and quotation that follow come from Apollodorus, who used Pherecydes; the myth, then, had this form by the early fifth century B.C.[54]

Acrisius learns from the oracle that his daughter, Danae, will give birth to a son who will kill him. Fearing that, he shuts her away in an underground chamber, but Zeus, changing himself into a shower of gold and streaming in through the roof, has intercourse with her. (Another version has it that Acrisius's brother, Proetus, seduced her.) When Acrisius finds out about the birth of Perseus, he puts both mother and son into a box and casts them into the sea. The box drifts to Cycladean Seriphus, where Dictys fishes it ashore and rears Perseus.

Dictys' brother, Polydectes, king of the island, desires Danae passionately but cannot have her because, the myth tells us, Perseus has grown to manhood. He therefore asks his friends, on the pretext of marriage to Hippodamia, for wedding presents. The others give horses, but Perseus boasts that he will fetch the gorgon's head, and Polydectes holds him to it.

Guided by Athena and Hermes, Perseus goes to the daughters of Phorcus, the Graeae, who have one eye and a single tooth which they pass among themselves. Perseus intercepts these and refuses to return them until the Graeae tell him where certain nymphs live. The nymphs give him winged sandals, a pouch, and Hades' cap of invisibility, and with these and a sickle obtained from Hermes, Perseus flies to the ocean and comes upon the gorgons sleeping.

The gorgons were Stheno, Euryale, and Medusa. Only Medusa was mortal, so Perseus was sent after her head. The gorgons had heads coiled about with serpents and great tusks like those of boars, bronze hands, and golden wings by which they flew.

They turned to stone any who looked at them. Perseus stood over them while they were sleeping. With Athena directing his hand, turning away and looking into a bronze shield in which he saw the gorgon's reflection, he cut off Medusa's head. When her head was severed, there leaped out the winged horse, Pegasus, and Chrysaor, father of Geryonos, Medusa's children by Poseidon.[55]

Perseus puts the head in the pouch and flees, escaping Medusa's pursuing sisters by using the cap of invisibility.

On the way back to Seriphus he finds Andromeda, daughter of the Ethiopian king, Cepheus, bound to a rock. Poseidon, in sympathy with the Nereids, whose beauty the king's wife, Cassiepea, insulted, has sent a flood and a monster. Although the oracle of Ammon has predicted a release from disaster if Cepheus's daughter is given to the monster, Perseus at first sight desires Andromeda and kills the monster on the promise of her hand in marriage. Afterward, he uses Medusa's head to turn Cepheus's brother, Phineus, into stone, since Phineus, who was supposed to marry Andromeda before Perseus's arrival, was plotting against him.

Perseus comes back to Seriphus to find his mother and Dictys suppliants at the altars in fear of Polydectes' violence. He turns Polydectes to stone and makes Dictys king in his place; then, through Hermes, he returns the sandals and cap to the nymphs and gives the gorgon's head to Athena, who displays it on her shield. After this, Perseus goes with Danae and Andromeda to Acrisius's city of Argos, but in terror of the oracle, Acrisius flees to Pelasgia. Perseus goes there to participate in athletic games and accidentally kills Acrisius with a discus. Ashamed to return to Argos, he exchanges kingships with Megapenthes of Tiryns and lives there with his mother and wife, by whom he has sons.

The provenance of the myth is still disputed by scholars, but it is clear that Perseus was not always associated with Medusa. Homer refers to both without mentioning the beheading, the event linking them. By the early sixth century B.C., however, the myth and the artistic representation of Medusa were in their classical form, so problems of development do not concern us here. The myth that Apollodorus and Pherecydes report is for the most part the one Aeschylus knew.[56]

The Perseus myth is told from the son's viewpoint, and the primary tension is between mother and son. The mother is split into two figures: Medusa, mother of Pegasus and Chrysaor, denotes her physical aspect, depicted as a terrifying monster; Danae embodies the mother as nurturing and supportive and so is represented in human terms. Medusa herself consists of two parts: the gorgon head and a body. The latter was certainly appended to the head later in the gorgon's history so that it could be slain.[57] The gorgon is clearly androgynous; it is a female and is given a female body, but its serpents, teeth, boar's tusks, pendent tongue, and occasional beard are male attributes.[58] The males in the myth are also split into two types: those that are sexually threatening to female figures; and Dictys, who supports Perseus. The aim of the myth is the suppression of the negative side of the mother, which it defines as her physical sexuality. For that reason the major motif of the myth is the dissociation of a whole into a positive and a negative aspect. On the narrative level this is worked out by slaying Medusa, preventing Danae from using her sexuality, and eliminating sexual males.

The first episode of the myth creates the ideal situation for the son: Perseus possesses his mother inside a box, an image of the womb but not a womb, floating on waters that symbolize the waters of the womb but are not those. He is not a fetus; he is born, conscious, and aware of his mother. He has escaped with her from male hostility represented by Acrisius, Zeus, and/or Proetus. Acrisius, afraid of him before his birth, acts against his mother. Acrisius's hostility is not sexual, which may explain why his death, unlike that of the other males, is unintentional. Since they achieve what the myth seeks to avert, Proetus is said to have "ruined" Danae and is never again mentioned, while Zeus is made remote— he does not even touch her with his body. Beyond the first necessary contact, sexual males are removed from Danae, thereby desexualizing her.

Perseus is raised by Dictys, whose name means "net." Though he is named for his part in the myth, the net is a female image. Perseus is reared by a male whose sexuality has been transferred to his brother and so is nonthreatening, even maternal. In this regard it is significant that Perseus does not give his mother to Dictys in marriage, the logical place for her "in the order of things."

That Polydectes cannot have Danae sexually because of Perseus's majority, which again "in the order of things" makes no sense, is the crux of the myth. He cannot have her because the mythmaker wants her virginal. Acrisius tries to prevent Perseus's conception; Proetus or Zeus, once he impregnates her, vanishes; Dictys is without sexuality, and the hypersexed Polydectes is killed.

Medusa and the gorgon represent the physical aspect of the mother. The gorgon is a "phallic mother" who took the father's penis for herself. Medusa expresses the same notion in that she carries within her the effect of Poseidon's penetration. Unlike the androgynous Clytemnestra, who embodies all aspects of the male and female, these figures embody the physical process of sexual intercourse leading to conception and birth. They must be slain because the purpose of the myth is the denial of birth from a female.

The female aspect dominates the gorgon's appearance, but it is the male in combination with it that signals the terror. The latter is killed twice: once with the beheading and again with the slaying of the monster sent by Poseidon. The monster—or Poseidon's sexuality displaced as a monster—intends to eat Andromeda, another possible sexual reference. Cassiepea's boast that she is more beautiful than the Nereids recalls Perseus's boastfulness at Polydectes' wedding feast, and both motivate the narrative, but what is afoot is the annihilation of the male side of the gorgon. Poseidon is more than Medusa's partner; he embodies the male side of the androgyne, which is killed in the form of his monster. That explains why Perseus does not use the gorgon against the monster: The monster *is* the serpents in another form.

Psychoanalysts since Ferenczi and Freud have interpreted the gorgon as the maternal genitalia, which, when seen by the son, arouse in him fears that his body might be so mutilated. The phallic serpents, Freud proposed, reassure the son of his own penis, and sight of the head counters castration fears with the stonelike condition of an erection. The difficulty with this view, as Philip E. Slater reasoned, is that it puts "the primary psychological significance of the female genital" in the male and makes the gorgon a defensive device for him. The serpents, he says, are a source of fear, not compensation. Slater concludes that the beheading is intended "to divest the mother of those male-envying and male-hating attributes which corrode the mother-son relationship."[59]

There is no doubt that the purpose of the myth is to divest the mother of *something* and that Slater is correct in making the serpents part of the terror of the gorgon. Fear of castration is an unlikely motive, however, when it is Perseus, "Cutter," who is divesting Medusa of her head, a head marked by elementary sexual symbols. Moreover, hero myths are constructed around three archetypal moments in every life—birth, coming of age, death—and not around daily events, as Slater's interpretation implies.[60] The Perseus myth attempts to deny birth from the sexual process and from the female. The gorgon represents sexual intercourse, the commingling of the sexes, as gross animality. To behead the gorgon is to cut away all that. The myth does the same thing in humanized form by keeping Danae from being sexual. The desideratum is Danae in the box—a virgin nurse, something impossible in the real world.

The mythmaker betrays the futility of his effort with the birth of Perseus, despite Acrisius's effort to avert it, and with Andromeda. The feminine whole cannot be fragmented and its parts suppressed, which is the aim of Athenian mythmaking. Any name could have served for the maiden on the rock. Andromeda is the "Ruler of Men," a name she shares with Medusa, "Ruler." Perseus kills one embodiment of sexual intercourse and ends up with another. Their latent identity comes out in the metamorphosis, beginning in the fourth century B.C., of Medusa into a beautiful woman.[61]

Perseus uses Medusa's head to protect Danae and Andromeda from sexual males. On Athena's shield it protects Athena's virginity. Once removed from Medusa's body and placed, not in Athena's body, but out on her shield in plain sight, the gorgon loses its ability to turn to stone any but the sexually violent. More to the point, on her shield it denotes Athena's lack of sexuality, for her androgyny is nonphysical. She has no part of marriage, intercourse, birth. Restored within her and combined with her military attributes, the gorgon would make of Athena an Amazon.

Clytemnestra as Gorgon

By the time the Chorus makes the analogy with Perseus, the audience is ready to accept Clytemnestra as a gorgon. Cassandra first speaks of her as a serpent in the *Agamemnon*. The action of the *Libation Bearers* is motivated by Clytemnestra's dream in which she gives birth to a serpent. She wraps it in swaddling clothes and puts it to her breast. It bites her and sucks blood with its milk. Orestes interprets the vision as follows:

> If the serpent left the same place as I and was dressed in the same clothes and took with open mouth the breast, source of my nourishment, and if sweet milk mixed with clots of blood and she cried out in fear over the pain, she is bound to die violently since she nourished a dreadful creature. I become a snake and kill her.[62]

The Chorus welcomes his reading and, after he has done the deed, praises him for "lopping off the heads of two serpents." Clytemnestra in her last words alive reaches the same conclusion: "I birthed and reared this one as serpent. My fear from these dreams foresaw the future."[63] Love between mother and son is replaced by imagery of blood-sucking serpents.

The Perseus myth endeavors to remove sexuality from the mother in order to make her solely a virginal nurse. In the ways of myths Medusa is done away with and Danae is turned into a virtual virgin. Aeschylus attains the identical solution using the tools of the dramatist. He confronts Orestes with Clytemnestra's sexuality and then moves her away from him as mother. Since sex is part of Clytemnestra, she must be dissociated from the mother. Orestes can kill his gorgon, but, unlike Perseus, he knows that he is born of her.

Even as Aeschylus asserts the kinship of Clytemnestra and Orestes using the serpent image, he is undermining it. The image, William Whallon rightly observes, "does not represent either person only, but becomes a symbol of the unnatural relationship between them."[64] Everything induces Orestes to interpret the dream as he does and to declare himself serpent. But Aeschylus intervenes in the Cilissa scene to contradict this reading: Cilissa, the slave, was his wetnurse, and she, not Clytemnestra, grieves his death. Orestes could not have bitten Clytemnestra's breast, for he suckled at Cilissa's. Rather, it is Clytemnestra's Erinyes who want to suck Orestes' blood.[65] The dream is a figment of Clytemnestra's serpentine nature; it is as false for Orestes as her holding out to him her breast as his place of suckling. To quote Whallon again:

> Thus the dream appears a false omen: Orestes cannot be thought the serpent in swaddling clothes to which Clytemnestra offered her breast, if she did not fill for him as a child this most tender office of a mother. The bond between them is loosened by the denial that an image connecting them is valid.[66]

The kinship is further attenuated by Apollo's priestess in the *Eumenides*. Orestes sees Clytemnestra's furies as resembling gorgons. The Pythia, too, notes this at first ("I do not mean women but gorgon-types"), but on second look she recants: "I will not liken them to gorgons." The gorgon of sexuality that is Clytemnestra is divorced from the mother's avenging spirits. Clytemnestra as gorgon vanishes altogether when Athena, seeing the Erinyes, asks who they are: "You are like to no race of the begotten, neither seen among the goddesses by the gods nor resembling the shape of mortal . . ." She breaks off: "right withdraws, and it is far from just for the blameless to insult neighbors."[67] They bear no resemblance to anything; they are unique—the avenging Erinyes of the Mother. Though they would look no different on stage, the shift in identity is overwhelming.

The gorgon dies to deny sexuality to the female as mother. The daring woman dies to deny the woman as wife and daughter a will of her own. Clytemnestra is easily eliminated as the one who "killed him she ought not to have killed." Her death as gorgon is more difficult because it is more crucial to the mythmaking and is a physical impossibility in the real world. Eurycleia, in the *Odyssey*, was the nurse of Telemachus, but Penelope is no less his mother.[68] It would be a rare queen in a society of slaves who would burden herself with a wetnurse's burden; Cilissa herself catalogs its inconveniences. Aeschylus would have us see one facet of mothering as the whole. When Clytemnestra holds out her breast, Aeschylus betrays how precarious is his denial of her motherhood. Stunned, Orestes turns to Pylades:

> *Orestes.* Pylades, what am I to do? Am I to be shamed from killing my mother?
> *Pylades.* Where, then, in the future are Apollo's prophecies uttered at Pytho and your pledges firmed by oaths? Count all your enemies rather than the gods.

Pylades has been standing beside Orestes during the whole play. The audience has by now discounted him as one of the silent players for which Aeschylus was well known.[69] When Pylades speaks, his words command the authority of Delphi itself. Yet Orestes asks again, this time of the Erinyes themselves, "Am I of my mother's blood?" The question stirs divine intervention in the affairs of mortals to deny them their most inalienable bond. Clytemnestra has been put away, and the gorgon of sex and daring volition suppressed. The aspects of unnatural wife and mother complement the marginal daughter represented by the Amazon to convey the total meaning of androgyny in Athenian mythmaking.

·CHAPTER 6·

The Meaning of the Amazon Myth

A FOUNDATION myth relates a past event that continues to shape the world it addresses. Such myths contrive and reveal  again and again a solution to a problem inherent in the social system. They should not be thought of as giving a final answer, one that removes the problem altogether. Moreover, they must be read in the context of the social structure and historical moment that informed them. The Amazons are said to have invaded Attica and to have been slaughtered because in classical Athens they existed expressly to die each time they were seen in paintings or their name was spoken. Their defeat did not permanently blot out the specter of an uprising by women against men. There was no need for a myth to explain the impossibility of such a revolution, for there was little likelihood that Athenian women would replace men as heads of families and state. But tensions over women and marriage with them had constantly to be relieved. As a foundation myth, the myth of the Amazons aided in dissipating those anxieties by supporting the sexual dichotomy institutionalized in Athenian marriage. The message of the myth had to be repeated and heard again and again because the problems of women and marriage could never be solved once and for all.

AMAZONS AND AUTOCHTHONY
IN FUNERAL ORATORY

After Xerxes' retreat, orators at state funerals developed a catalog of exploits whose purpose was to disguise Athenian imperialism as service to other Greeks and to smooth over the contradiction between the Athenians' claim to be defenders of Greek freedom and their growing suppression of it. Among the services they boasted of were the defense of Athens against the Amazons, the recovery of the Argive corpses at Thebes, the expulsion of Eumolpus and the Thracians from Greece, and the succoring of Heracles' children. These events were taken to prove another claim of the orators: that the Athenians were autochthonous. The funeral oration attributed to Demosthenes, which he may have delivered in 338 B.C. over the dead of Chaeronea, illustrates the formulaic connection between autochthony and the catalog:

> The noble birth of these men has been acknowledged among
> all mankind from time immemorial. Not only is it possible
> for them and every one of their ancestors to refer their phys-
> ical nature to their father; they can also trace it back to the
> whole fatherland which they hold in common and from
> which, it is admitted, they are born. They alone of all man-
> kind inhabit the land from which they sprang and passed it
> on to their descendants. The following assumption may
> thus be made: Those who came into their cities from else-
> where and were called citizens are like adopted children.
> These men [to whom the oration is dedicated] are legitimate
> children born of the seed of their fatherland. That the fruits
> by which mankind lives first appeared among us, in addi-
> tion to being the most important service to all, seems to me
> to be a self-evident sign that our land is the mother of our
> ancestors. For all things that give birth provide by their na-
> ture nourishment for their offspring. This the land has
> done. . . . The ancestors, fathers, and grandfathers of the

present generation never wronged any Greek or foreigner. Besides their other noble and brave qualities it was their nature to be the most just. For they conquered the host of the Amazons when it came, expelling them beyond the Phasis River. [1]

The Athenians, then, were born of the earth, which gave them a mother's nourishment. In other versions the earth also gave them gods, skills, and weapons. [2] Because of their autochthony they could never, by definition, deprive another of his land and so are just by nature. Lysias puts the claim succinctly:

In many ways it was natural for our ancestors to fight with a single purpose over justice. For the beginning of their life was just. They were not collected from all parts, like the many, nor did they expel others and inhabit a foreign land. Born of the earth herself, they possessed the same land as mother and fatherland. [3]

Pericles' funeral oration exemplifies the flow of the argument from autochthony, here rationalized as continuous habitation, to expansionism and "defensive" imperialism:

These men dwelled in this land always in a succession of generations until the present one and handed it over free because of their bravery. They are worthy of praise, and still more are our fathers. Having possessed, in addition to what they inherited, as much empire as we have, they passed it on to us not without toil. We ourselves, those now in the settled stage of life, have increased most parts of it and have made the city self-sufficient both for war and peace. Their deeds in wars by which each possession was obtained, whether we or our fathers defended against the foreigner or hostile Greek, I shall omit since I am unwilling to boast among those who know for themselves. [4]

The argument autochthony–just nature–just imperialism makes little sense. Only nonsense could gloss over the obvious, but what is significant here is the way the Athenians glossed it over. They reassured themselves of their just nature by denying birth from the womb. Plato, in the *Menexenos,* provides a parallel instance of the reasoning that clarifies what is not being said:

> So firm and healthy are the nobility and freedom of the city
> and the natural hatred of barbarians among us because we
> are pure Greeks, unmixed with barbarians. The descendants
> of Pelops, Cadmus, Aegyptus, Danaus, and many others
> live with us, being barbarian by nature and Greek by custom
> only. We ourselves are Greeks and live unmixed with bar-
> barians. Consequently, there is instilled in us a hatred of the
> foreign nature.[5]

Free of the taint of the foreigner, Athenians are strong and healthy. Others came to Greece with barbarian blood, but the Athenians' nobility—that is, their autochthony—keeps them pure.

By now the identification in Athenian mythmaking of barbarian with women and weakness is familiar. What could not be said openly about women is said in terms of Asians. The Amazon myth in funeral oratory proved the purity of the men of Athens from the "foreign" nature of women: The Athenians are not born of woman. For a short while even Socrates felt the glow of the message of the funeral oration:

> The speech resounded so, and the speaker's voice filled my
> ears. Three or four days later I remembered who I was and
> where on earth I was—then it was not easy. In the meantime
> I thought that I was living on the islands of the Blessed.[6]

On those islands in the West there are no women, and men dine with the gods and become gods—the way it was before Pandora.[7]

AUTOCHTHONY AND BIRTH IN THE ORESTEIA

The earliest mention of Athenian autochthony, dating perhaps to the sixth century B.C., refers to king Erechtheus, "whom Athena, daughter of Zeus, nursed, and the grain-giving land birthed."

Funeral orators were the first to extend birth from their soil to all Athenians, and Euripides introduced the claim into tragedy with the *Erechtheus* (c. 422 B.C.).[8] But before Euripides, Aeschylus had absorbed the message of autochthony and conveyed it in the *Oresteia.*

After Athena persuades the Erinyes to depart from their wrath over Orestes' acquittal, they stand before her awaiting instructions on how best to praise her city:

> *Erinyes.* What song do you bid we sing for this land?
> *Athena.* Sing of victory not ignobly won and of things from
>   the earth, dewy sea, and the heavens, and that the breath
>   of the winds blowing beneath the full sunshine come to the
>   land. Sing of the abundant produce of earth and beasts
>   which thrives for citizens—pray that it not grow weary with
>   time—and of the preservation of human seed. Be one to
>   cast out the impious. Like a gardener tending his plants, I
>   love this race of just men free of grief. Such things are
>   yours.[9]

By comparing Athena to a gardener (literally, a tender of plants), Aeschylus re-creates the mystery of Athenian myth-making. Athena overcomes reality, which must be surmounted if her worshipers are to transcend their existence. The simile functions as a metaphor, for the Athenians *are* plants, children of the earth, whose fertility is promoted by virgin Erinyes and tended by the virgin Athena, who, as her choice of words indicates,[10] loves them with the love of a parent. Hers is precisely the role ascribed to the mother as protector of the plant/child by Apollo in his lesson on "embryology."[11] With little dramatic provocation she then pronounces them "a race of just men free of grief," for which the only justification can be their autochthony.[12]

Critics have had trouble with this line because they expect a reference to gardening. Their literary intuition is sound, but Aeschylus is making more than poetry. For him, plants and gardeners are tied to the earth, more or less closely, so that they may be regarded as contiguous with generation from the earth.

They are metonyms for such birth, just as the crown is for kingship. The crown is a sign in that it is literally part of kingship.[13]
As crown proves kingship, so the plant and gardener in this context, viewed as part of birth from the earth, prove the factuality
of that birth. "Just" in Athena's pronouncement refers, therefore, not to judicial justice but to the metaphysical justice of
birth from "not-woman."

The *Libation Bearers* closes with the death of the tyrants,
Clytemnestra and Aegisthus, and with the exile of the legitimate
heir to the kingship, Orestes. Movement toward a new order has
already begun as Orestes leaves for Delphi and purification by
Apollo. From there he goes to Athens, and Athena, confronted
with the dilemma of choosing between the Erinyes' claim on
Orestes for matricide and his duty to his father and throne, puts
herself above the necessity of choice by establishing a court.
Henceforth, justice is determined not by the family vendetta of
cyclical murder, but by a public organ of disinterested judges.
The male court oversees breaches in the public sphere while the
Erinyes-become-August Ones maintain the fertility and prosperity
of the family and city.

As mythmaking, however, all this must be appreciated as an
apparatus for escaping birth from woman. The justice of the trial
is not reasoned; he who has confessed matricide is set free by the
vote of Athena, who casts her ballot out of prejudice against
women and everything female. Aeschylus is not depicting a moment in the past, nor is he instructing his audience on evolution
in society, morals, or justice. He is giving the Athenians a fantasy
of their own purity and goodness, which we can penetrate only by
looking at what Aeschylus the mythmaker does on the stage.

Judicial justice mediates through words and deeds between the
problem of the woman who killed her husband with a right nag-
gingly undeniable and the need to escape the evils of the womb.
Considering the ostensible importance of justice and the trial of
the trilogy, it seems perverse of Aeschylus to have invented his
own etymology for Areopagus:

This is the hill of Ares, where the Amazons pitched their
tents when they came with an army in spite toward Theseus
and built towers against this new, lofty-towered city. They
sacrificed to Ares, thus giving his name to the rock.

The traditional etymology from Ares' trial there for homicide far
better fits a play about justice.[14] But Aeschylus's version signals
the nature of the court; it is the place where the female whole is
maimed, the problem of the negative aspects is surmounted, and
the evils of the womb are escaped. In other words, it is where the
female is stripped away, leaving the feminine.[15] Aeschylus's court
is the realization of a dream, the founding of a pure race of just
men.

The *Agamemnon* and the *Libation Bearers* correspond to each
other as strophe to antistrophe: the murder of Agamemnon is
answered by the murder of Agamemnon's murderers.[16] The *Eumenides* is outside their dialogue, unique, a new beginning. In this
play Aeschylus combines with utmost originality dramatic and
mythmaking strategies to solve the problem of women. In effect,
he responds to Hippolytus's lament, "O Zeus, if you wanted to
sow human seed, you ought not to have provided the means
from women," by constructing birth from not-woman. Athenians
could no more escape birth from the womb than they could, like
Piseterus in Aristophanes' *Birds,* build a city in the sky, but for a
moment they become the children of virgins, triumphing over
the womb.

From the outset Aeschylus distinguishes between Clytemnestra
the sexual, willful killer of husband and father and Clytemnestra
the mother slain by her son. The former appeared in the *Libation
Bearers* as a gorgon, and Orestes describes the Erinyes in that play
as "like gorgons, black-robed and entwined with many serpents."
Yet the Pythia, in doubt, does not see serpents, and Athena refuses
to speculate on their looks. Aeschylus speaks away the gorgon that
was Clytemnestra. The Erinyes' concern for justice moves them
still further away from the Clytemnestra who seeks physical pain

and torment for Orestes.[17] The Erinyes are the furies of the mother, not Clytemnestra, which explains why they fail to avenge her as they do the other dead: "You sleep? What good are you to me asleep?" Clytemnestra complains. "I am dishonored by you among the dead."[18] This scene follows upon Apollo's promise to Orestes of salvation; the god will rescue Orestes, but the furies will avenge, not Clytemnestra, but the mother.

Aeschylus polarizes male and female at Delphi through sight and sound. Apollo and Orestes walk together onto the stage; Apollo appears in human form, likely more splendidly dressed than Orestes; during their entrance they are speaking together in straightforward Greek. The Erinyes, on the other hand, probably enter sporadically and in disarray; they are hideous, bestial apparitions; before entering they were groaning; now they sing dark obscurities and dance (wildly?).[19] Sight and sound serve to contrast the sexes, creating a polarity which is intensified by the fact that Apollo and the Erinyes are not brought together until line 179; Orestes and the Erinyes, not until line 585.

During the flurry of the prologue, however, Aeschylus lays down the principle held in common by the opposing parties, and when finally Apollo and the Erinyes confront one another at Delphi, they use the same language, though they mean different things by it. As they contest the central issue of the marriage tie versus kinblood, Apollo refers to the justice of the conjugal bed and the Erinyes to the justice of their pursuit of Orestes.[20] With justice established as the rationale for the trial, the action shifts to Athens; the mythmaking, to the collusion of Athena and the Erinyes.

In the preliminary questioning before Athena the Erinyes accuse Orestes of matricide and blame him for not giving an oath affirming his innocence. Since Orestes has admitted his guilt, Athena rejects the procedure of an oath. She does so out of regard for the circumstances rather than the facts of the case:

Athena. Do you wish to be just in reputation or do you want to act according to justice?

Erinyes. How is that? Instruct me. You are not deficient in
wisdom.

Athena. I say do not let the unjust prevail by oaths.

Erinyes. Well, question him, and give a straight judgment.

Athena. Would you entrust the outcome of the accusation to
me?

Erinyes. Certainly. We respect you and receive respect in
return.[21]

This is the turning point in Aeschylus's mythmaking: Athena in
her wisdom, the wisdom of her father Zeus, is about to consider
the problem of the female *with her consent.* Through the trial,
Aeschylus translates the problem from a social conflict between
the sexes into a deliberation of judicial and political issues. These
are matters in which the reasoning men of the jury can determine
what they want. The Erinyes become prosecutors, Orestes the
defendant, Apollo his advocate, and Athena the presiding magis-
trate, who dictates procedure as the trial unfolds. Her "wisdom"
is Aeschylus's mediation, through the metaphor of the trial, of
society's dependence upon female fertility and its fear of female
rashness and sexuality.

The Erinyes begin by cross-examining Orestes, who admits his
guilt. Clytemnestra had "two strokes of pollution upon her," he
argues, "for she killed her husband and my father. Why did you
not drive her into exile?" The Erinyes reply: "She was not of
the same blood as the man she killed."[22] Then Orestes asks the
question which, more than his case, it is the function of the court
to settle: "Am I of my mother's blood?" The Erinyes respond
with what appears to be the incontrovertible fact of human existence: "Of course. Did she not nourish you beneath her girdle?
Are you repudiating the dearest blood of your mother?"[23] Orestes
was carried beneath Clytemnestra's girdle. If the case turns on that
alone, as the Erinyes believe it should, escape from the mother is
impossible. But Aeschylus shifts the issue to *the blood link* between mother and son. If it can be shown that the son is not of his
mother's blood, then, despite the fact that Clytemnestra carried

him, he killed her in righteous vengeance for killing his true parent, the father. That is, he will be shown to be a just man not only legally but metaphysically.

Baffled as to whether he acted justly or not—that is, whether he is of his mother's blood—Orestes turns to Apollo for testimony and explanation. On the basis of his authority as Zeus's infallible prophet, Apollo affirms that the deed was justly done. The order to slay Clytemnestra, he says, originated with Zeus, since she murdered one of his scepter-bearing kings. Apollo then cites the theory of embryology which reduces the mother to caretaker of the father's and sole parent's seed. Finally, he directs the attention of the jurors to Athena as "proof" that "there may be a father without a mother."

The voting that now takes place, another critical step in the mythmaking, was as evident to the spectators that day in Elaphebolion (March) as it is perplexing to those who today have only the script. With a reminder to observe their oath, Athena instructs the jurors to take up their voting pebbles and decide the case. There follows a couplet spoken by the Erinyes and then one by Apollo. Four more alternations ensue, with the Erinyes' final couplet extended to a triplet; the Erinyes have spoken six times, Apollo five. Then Athena declares the following:

> This is my task: to decide the case last. I will add this pebble
> for Orestes. There is no mother at all who bore me. I praise
> the male in all things wholeheartedly excepting marriage. I am
> exceedingly my father's. Thus I shall not prefer the fate of
> a woman who killed the man, overseer of the house. Orestes
> wins should the case be judged by equal votes.[24]

Athena, without doubt, casts a vote by putting her pebble in the urn for acquittal: "I will add this pebble for Orestes." Whether her vote made or broke a tie among jurors has often vexed scholars, but the construction of the scene dictates that she creates a tie.[25] With each couplet spoken by Apollo, a juror, we may suppose, came forward and voted for acquittal, while the couplets and final triplet spoken by the Erinyes accounted for six votes for condemnation. The triplet gives Athena time to come forward and pronounce the grounds for her vote and the ruling on a tie. The fact that her vote results in the tie means that even Apollo's argumentation and Athena's presence failed to convince a plurality of the jurors, who voted six to five for mother's blood, despite the enormity of Clytemnestra's deed.[26] But by her vote and ruling, Athena (i.e., Aeschylus) imposes upon them birth from not-woman. Even as Aeschylus's jurors revere the mother, they are forced by their goddess to deny her bond with her children. Clytemnestra is dismissed, a faithless wife and a common murderer, for if she is not Orestes' mother, neither is she Iphigenia's.[27]

With the verdict the trial and the Erinyes' suit for justice are completed. The Erinyes continue to be angry, but no longer for Clytemnestra's sake; she is forgotten. In the scene that follows, Athena faces spirits of the mother enraged over what they perceive as an injury to their prerogatives:

> Younger gods, you have ridden roughshod over ancient laws
> and snatched him [Orestes] from my hands. But I, dis-
> honored, wretched, grievous in wrath, am in this land and
> shall send on the earth in return for my heart's suffering
> a dripping unbearable. A blight—no leaves, no children—
> rushing over the land—O Justice—shall cast in the land man-
> slaughtering stains.[28]

Athena persuades the Erinyes to let go of their wrath and become resident aliens at Athens, dwelling in chambers beneath the Areopagus. For "chambers" Aeschylus uses the word *thalamoi*, which denotes the women's quarters of the house. Aeschylus thus has Athena introduce the Erinyes into the "household" of Athens. Their dowry—the first fruits of the harvest and sacrifices for weddings and births—is given to them by the people of Attica.

Athena, virgin warrior and motherless daughter of the father, and the Erinyes, fertility virgins and fatherless daughters of the mother, are complements. Together they represent the virgin who is loyal to her father and whose fertility is available to him without his having to give her away in marriage. Because the Erinyes have no father, they have no allegiance to another household and thus provide without reservation the fertility of Athens, perpetuating it with members and sustenance. These functions are normally embodied in the wife as the metaphorical field for the husband's plowing. Since they are now fulfilled by virgins without sexual intercourse, there is no need to bring in a wife, a situation whose dangers and potential for pollution are illustrated by Clytemnestra. "May no such wife live with me," Orestes prays. "Sooner may I die childless at the gods' doing." The house of Athens is self-sufficient, free of the taint and problem of the sexed woman, whose nature is foreign in physique, blood, and loyalties.

The social equivalent of the construct Athena-Erinyes is the *epikleros,* a girl whose father dies without leaving a male heir.[29] The girl is married to her nearest relative on her father's side, and the son of that union, the father's grandson, inherits his property. Insofar as the purpose of the institution of the *epikleros* was the same as that of marriage—namely, to keep alive the father's house—he (the grandson) is, in effect, the father's son by his own daughter. What is prohibited in practice by taboo on incest is realized in the Athena-Erinyes construct: Athena embodies the *epikleros*'s loyalty to her father, and the Erinyes embody her reproductivity. Together they make a whole—the *epikleros.* Their separate appearances on stage belie the fact that, given the model of the *epikleros,* Athena makes available to the house of Athens her own reproductivity. Athenians are born and not born from their own virgin goddess—"born" in the sense that it is her reproductivity that sustains the house of Athens, yet "not born" in that her reproductivity has been displaced to the Erinyes. Athena-Erinyes as not-woman is more than a figment of Aeschylus's imagination; it is a poetic realization of the optimum in the marriage system. The mythmaker has solved the problem of women by abrogating the need to bring them into the house and, more importantly, by annulling their role as generators of life.

AN INTERPRETATION

The Amazon myth explains something troubling about the status quo in classical Athens in three fundamental areas: the military, the religious, and the marital. In the first it explains the Athenians' victory in the Persian wars and later the righteousness of their imperialism. In the religious area it explains an aspect of the goddess Athena for the men of Pericles' generation. In the final area the myth explains patriarchal marriage as the optimum means for controlling female sexuality and rashness and, in particular, the necessity that the daughter be given away in marriage. The first of these areas has been discussed in previous chapters, and what has been said need not be repeated.

Possession of an empire undermined the ethnocentricity that unified and closed off the Athenian *polis* from others. Athenian soldiers fought no longer just at their borders but all over the Mediterranean, and they brought home knowledge of other customs and peoples. The state's dependence upon a wide base of citizens for fighters and rowers supported leaders whose policies moved government away from the traditional aristocracy toward ever more radical democracy. Wealth, siphoned into the city as tribute, attracted philosophers, artists, and businessmen. Products from around the empire were sold in the agora. At the same time, fear and hatred of Athenian imperialism and the uncertainty of change and isolation must have been widespread in the city. Athenians turned to their goddess, Athena, as the focal point for a national identity. They projected through her the image they would have of themselves. Part of that image is explained by the Amazon myth. The historical process that changed Athena the *Potnia*, or "lady," of the Mycenean civilization into Athena the virgin-warrior deity of the Homeric and later periods culminated in a liminal figure very like the Amazon.[30] The Amazon myth explained Athena as a warrior-virgin who was not threatening; the violence and chaos of her liminality—that is, the notion that the daughter would use her own productivity, protected by her own

military might, to found her own household and city—had been
excised in the death of her surrogates, the Amazons.

As seen in Chapter One, the foremost monument to Athena as
the goddess of Pericles' generation was the Parthenon, in whose
sculpture the Amazon myth appears prominently. Athena's success in the contest with Poseidon as depicted in the west pediment was meant to be balanced by the defeat of the Amazons
shown in the metope. Another Amazonomachy appeared around
a gorgon on the outer surface of the goddess's cult statue.[31] The
beginning of the battle is represented at the bottom of Athena's
shield, where one Greek, presumably Theseus, has already killed
his Amazon. Up the right side the fighting is fierce and the issue
is in doubt. At the top are three defenders, the center one being
a bald old man who is hurling a rock down at an Amazon. Evelyn
B. Harrison identifies these figures as three generations of autochthonous Attic kings, Cecrops, Erechtheus, and Pandion: "They
take part in this battle as Theseus took part in the battle of Marathon, rising from their graves to defend their native soil."[32] The
land itself—for Cecrops and the others are not old men in graves
but are avatars of the Attic soil—rises up to reject the Amazons.
Down the left side the Amazons are in rout, and the battle is
won.

Every interpretation of a symbol is tentative, but with Aeschylus as a guide, one will be ventured here.[33] The shield depicts the
"non-sense" of birth from not-woman; the Amazons are opposed
to the autochthonous kings directly and to Athena indirectly. The
shield graphically verifies the claim of funeral oratory: Athenians
are autochthonous, for, like their kings, they killed Amazons and
so reaffirmed their birthright. In the persons of the autochthonous
kings the Athenians' earth aids them against the female aberra-
tions of order. The death of the Amazons, since they are a reflex
of Athena, serves to aggregate her into the land by "pacifying"
her liminality.

The gorgon stares from the shield with the fascination of
nihility. The terror of that visage is Athena's reproductivity, her
sexuality. Aeschylus's Athena makes her reproductivity available

to the house of Athens through her complement, the Erinyes. In the *Ion* (c. 418 or 417 B.C.) Euripides refers to a myth that told how Earth bore the gorgon to support her children, the Giants, in the war against the Olympians. Athena slew it and made a breastplate out of its hide, the aegis. The latter detail is likely an invention, but the gorgon's autochthony and manner of death are not.[34] The slayer of the gorgon in later mythology, Perseus, was not always part of the myth. As the Amazons' death removed the military threat of Athena's liminality, so perhaps through the slaying of the gorgon the mythmaker divested Athena's liminality of its sexual component. The shield is a symbol, and here we tread the ground of speculation, but there is a certain sense about it: no one could deprive a mother goddess of her sexuality except the mother herself.

The desideratum of every Greek household was self-sufficiency.[35] None could achieve it because every house had to give out its daughters in marriage in order to receive others for its sons. The moment of separation, long foreseen and painful, was built into the social fabric. Personal tensions aside, however, and short of incest, the house would perish unless it relented. In a society of households jealous of their independence and suspicious of the women brought into the houses, exchange of daughters was an inescapable dilemma. The Amazon, the liminal figure of transition rites whose world is the reversal of all that is valued by the male, explains the necessity of the daughter to marry by portraying the consequences of her not marrying. The daughter must be given away by the father, and he must compromise the self-sufficiency of his household, so that order may be maintained on earth and in the cosmos. The message of the Amazon myth in the marital area is that the daughter must marry.

A female warrior or Amazon is not an impossibility; the plausibility of such a figure, in fact, has fortified those who would believe her real. But everything in the present study indicates that the Amazon is one permutation in a mythmaking based on the institution of marriage. The uniqueness of the Amazon is the reversal of the gender roles of marriage to create a female warrior.

Since in Athenian polar thinking such a figure could only dominate men, the principle of reversal is extended to define the female
cosmos of the Amazon. Moreover, since a female warrior is a contradiction in terms from the viewpoint of patriarchal marriage, the
Amazon is a hybrid, neither male (for the Amazon is female) nor
female (for the Amazon is a warrior): on the one hand, a liminal
figure in transition rites, the daughter who assumes the boy's
adult role; on the other hand, an androgyne whose strength sur-
passes that of single-sexed males. Thus the myth emphasizes the
death of Amazons in individual combat, rape, and mass slaughter.
In the myth of Heracles' Ninth Labor the Amazon's male side is
defeated by the male hero; in Theseus's rape of an Amazon the
female side is humbled. Annihilation before the Acropolis justified
Athenian imperialism in funeral oratory and, it seems likely,
aggregated the Athena of the Parthenon. But throughout the
myth's history the Amazon functioned to explain the imperative
that daughters must be given away and received into the house,
whatever the suffering or dangers such exchanges entailed. The
Amazon is a figment of Greek, and particularly Athenian, mythmaking concerning marriage. Those today who would make more
of it must do so in the awareness of their own mythmaking.

Notes

INTRODUCTION

1. The Amazons began, it has been suggested, as "a beardless small-statured race of bow-toting mongoloids" (K. A. Bisset, "Who Were the Amazons?" *Greece and Rome* 18 [1971]: 150–151); as Hittites (Walther Leonard, *Het-titer und Amazonen* [Leipzig; B. G. Teubner, 1911]); as female defenders of the shrines of the Great Mother against patriarchal invaders from the North (Merlin Stone, *When God Was a Woman* [New York: Dial, 1976], 46); as priestesses of the moon goddess (Robert Graves, *The Greek Myths: 1* [Baltimore: Penguin Books, 1960], 355); or as primitive communists who threw off the yoke of male slavery (Emanuel Kanter, *The Amazons: A Marxian Study* [Chicago: Charles H. Kerr, 1926]). For sources of the myth see H. Steuding, in Roscher, *Lex.* I, 267–280, s.v. *Amazonen;* J. Toepffer, *PW* I, 1754–1771, s.v. *Amazones;* Bernice Schultz Engle, "The Amazons in Ancient Greece," *The Psychoanalytic Quarterly* 11 (1942): 512–554.

2. For a study of polarity in Greek thought see G. E. R. Lloyd, *Polarity and Analogy* (Cambridge: Cambridge University Press, 1966), 15–171. For this mythmaking see, in particular, Sherry B. Ortner, "Is Female to Male as Nature Is to Culture?" in *Woman, Culture, and Society,* ed. Rosaldo and Lamphere, 67–87.

3. Zeitlin, "The Dynamics of Misogyny," 149–150:

> Moreover, the basic issue in the trilogy is the establishment in the face of female resistance of the binding nature of patriarchal marriage where wife's subordination and patrilineal succession are reaffirmed. In the course of the drama, in fact, every permutation of the feminine is exhibited before us: goddess, queen, wife, mother, daughter, sister, bride, virgin, adulteress, nurse, witch, Fury, priestess. Every issue, every action,

stems from the female so that she serves as the catalyst of events even as she is the main object of inquiry.

Zeitlin's is an insightful and provocative study of the techniques of myth-making in the *Oresteia*. Other works I have found particularly useful are Winnington-Ingram, "Clytemnestra and the Vote of Athena," 130–147; Zeitlin, "The Motif of the Corrupted Sacrifice in Aeschylus' *Oresteia*," 463–508; and Lebeck, *The Oresteia*. The Greek texts for the *Oresteia* are Gilbertus Murray, *Aeschyli septem quae supersunt tragoediae*, 2nd ed. (Oxford: Oxford University Press, 1955); and Denys Page, *Aeschylus: Agamemnon* (Oxford: Oxford University Press, 1957). I have noted those instances where I have adopted a different reading.

4. For this view of tragedy see Jean-Pierre Vernant, "Tensions and Ambiguities in Greek Tragedy," in *Interpretation: Theory and Practice,* ed. Charles S. Singelton (Baltimore: Johns Hopkins Press, 1969), 105–121; idem, "Greek Tragedy: Problems of Interpretation," in *The Languages of Criticism and the Sciences of Man,* ed. Richard Macksey and Eugenio Donato (Baltimore: Johns Hopkins Press, 1970), 273–289; idem, "Ambiguïté et renversement," 101–131; idem, "Hestia-Hermès," 124–170; John Jones, *On Aristotle and Greek Tragedy* (London: Chatto and Windus, 1971), 11–62; Segal, "The Raw and the Cooked in Greek Literature," 289–308; idem, *Tragedy and Civilization,* 13–59; James M. Redfield, *Nature and Culture in the* Iliad: *The Tragedy of Hector* (Chicago: University of Chicago Press, 1975), 45–91.

CHAPTER 1

1. Arr. *Anab.* 7.13.4–5.

2. This sentence is a paraphrase of Bothmer, *Amazons,* 6.

3. Bothmer, *Amazons,* 7 (vase 19), 14, and pl. X.

4. Eur. *HF* 408–418; the text is corrupt from "to get" to "daughter." See also Ap. Rhod. 2.964–969; Diod. 4.16; Paus. 1.2.1; Apollod. *Bibl.* 2.5.9; Schol. Pind. *Nem.* 3.38; Just. *Epit.* 2.4; Robert, *Heldensage,* 2:462–465 and 558–561. Apollodorus's version is quoted in Chapter Five above.

5. Robert, *Heldensage,* 2:465, notes that Heracles must have gone on his own in an earlier version.

6. Bothmer, *Amazons,* 15 and pl. II, 1.

7. John Boardman, "Herakles, Peisistratos, and Sons," *Rev. Arch.* (1972): 57–72; idem, "Herakles, Peisistratos, and Eleusis," *JHS* 95 (1975): 1–12.

8. Webster, *Potter and Patron in Classical Athens,* 259; Boardman, *Athenian Black Figure Vases,* 221–223; idem, *Athenian Red Figure Vases,* 11–15 and 226–228.

9. Nilsson, *The Mycenaean Origin of Greek Mythology,* 170–176; Hom. *Il.* 2.552–556.

10. Thuc. 2.15.1–2; Plut. *Thes.* 24–25; Arist. *Ath. Pol.* 41; Robert, *Heldensage,* 2:749–755; Herter, "Theseus der Athener," 284–286; idem, "Theseus," 1046; Karl Schefold, "Kleisthenes," *MH* 3 (1964): 65–67; Felix Jacoby, *Atthis: The Local Chronicles of Ancient Athens* (Oxford: Oxford University Press, 1949), 394, n. 20; idem, *FGrH* 3 b 309–311, 3 b II 343, n. 23, and 3 b II 344, n. 20; Connor, "Theseus in Classical Athens," 144–152; Webster, *Potter and Patron in Classical Athens,* 74–75 and 252–253.

11. It seems more likely that the myths were developed over a long period of time (Barrett, *Euripides: Hippolytus,* 3, n. 1) rather than appearing wholecloth in one *Theseis* during the last decades of the sixth century (Jacoby, *FGrH* 3 b II 344, n. 20). The *Theseis* was an episodic poem that listed Theseus's adventures (Arist. *Poet.* 1451 a 16–22). On the scant evidence for the *Theseis* see G. L. Huxley, *Greek Epic Poetry from Eumelos to Panyassis* (Cambridge: Harvard University Press, 1969), 116–118.

12. Pind. fr. 175; Pherec. fr. 151 in Jacoby, *FGrH* I A 98; Hellanicus fr. 16 in *FGrH* 3 B 45; Herodorus fr. 25a in *FGrH* 1.220; Istrus fr. 10 in *FGrH* 3 B 171; Plut. *Thes.* 28–29; Apollod. *Epit.* 1.16–17 and 5.2.

13. If Theseus did not obtain an Amazon wife by rape, another means had to be postulated. Philochorus suggested that Theseus received her from Heracles as a prize of war (Put. *Thes.* 26.1; also Diod. 4.16.1). Others have her fall in love with Theseus and go willingly (Hegias in Paus. 1.2.1; Isoc. 12.193). See Robert, *Heldensage,* 2: 730–731; and Jacoby, *FGrH* 3 b 437.

14. Istrus fr. 10 in Jacoby, *FGrH* 3 B 171; Plut. *Thes.* 8.4–5; Nilsson, *The Mycenaean Origin of Greek Mythology,* 164–65.

15. Jacoby, *FGrH* 3 b 439–440; Herter, "Theseus," 1149–1150.

16. Cleidemus fr. 18 in Jacoby, *FGrH* 3 B 56–57. Cleidemus may have invented this conclusion to the war by connecting the Horcomosium, a place near the Theseum named after an oath (*horkos*), with the Amazon invasion.

17. Jacoby, *FGrH* 3 b 74–75. Cleidemus replaced Theseus's voyage to Crete with the other youths by devising an expedition of King Theseus against Minos's sons and attributed to Theseus the suppression of piracy, traditionally an accomplishment of Minos (Thuc. 1.4.1).

18. Plut. *Thes.* 28.1.

19. Apollod. *Epit.* 1.21 and Chapter Five above.

20. Pind. fr. 176; Eur. *Hipp.* 307–309; Herter, "Theseus," 1153; Barrett, *Euripides: Hippolytus,* 8–9.

21. Hdt. 5.62–65; Thuc. 6.59.4; Arist. *Ath. Pol.* 19. For the treasury see Bothmer, *Amazons,* 117–119; for the dating of the treasury to 510–500 B.C. see William Bell Dinsmoor, "The Athenian Treasury as Dated by Its Ornament," *AJA* 50 (1946): 111–113.

22. Hdt. 5.63.

23. Hdt. 5.74-77; Andrew Robert Burn, *Persia and the Greeks* (London: Edward Arnold, 1962), 188-190.

24. Hdt. 1.62.1, 6.100; John L. Myres, *Herodotus, Father of History* (1953; Chicago: Henry Regnery, 1971), 182-183.

25. Bothmer, *Amazons,* 125 (vase 9), 128-129, and pl. LXVIII, 5.

26. Hdt. 1.87.1-2; for an illustration of Croesus on the pyre see Boardman, *Athenian Red Figure Vases,* illust. 171.

27. Webster, *Potter and Patron in Classical Athens,* 74-75; Hdt. 6.125.

28. Pherec. fr. 15 in Jacoby, *FGrH* I A 64, and fr. 151 and 152 in *FGrH* I A 98. For the date see Felix Jacoby, "The First Athenian Prose Writer," *Mnemos.* 13 (1947): 25-48, esp. 33.

29. For an account of the period and the years immediately following the wars see Ehrenberg, *From Solon to Socrates,* 122-191.

30. Thuc. 1.98.2; Diod. 4.62.4; Plut. *Cim.* 8.3-7; Paus. 1.17.2; Harp., s.v. *Polygnotus;* Schol. Ar. *Plut.* 627; Herter, "Theseus der Athener," 292-297; Connor, "Theseus," 157-160. This date for the fall of Scyros is based upon Plutarch's (*Thes.* 36.1) dating of the oracle to the archonship of Phaedon, given by Diodorus (11.48.1) as 476/75 B.C., and assumes that both oracle and capture were meant by Plutarch. Later dates for the capture have been suggested by J. D. Smart ("Kimon's Capture of Eion," *JHS* 87 [1967]: 136-138: 469/68 B.C.) and A. J. Podlecki ("Cimon, Skyros, and 'Theseus' Bones'," *JHS* 91 [1971]: 141-43; c. 470 B.C.), but neither is as persuasive as John P. Barron's ("New Light on Old Walls: The Murals of the Theseion," 20, n. 4, and 21, n. 7) counterarguments. The site of the Theseum has not been located and is known only from literary sources, for which see Judeich, *Topographie von Athen,* 351-353; and Wycherley, *The Athenian Agora III,* 113-119.

31. Pausanias (1.17.4), while identifying three paintings (Amazonomachy, Centauromachy, recovery of Minos's ring), mentions the release of Theseus by Heracles without referring to a painting. Barron ("New Light on Old Walls," 41-44) proposed that Pausanias neglected to state the subject of a fourth painting, the return from the underworld, which inspired the discussion of Theseus's death.

32. Plut. *Thes.* 27.7-8; Deubner, *Attische Feste,* 225.

33. Schol. Dem. 20.112; Paus. 1.15; Ar. *Lys.* 677-679 and Schol. on *Lys.* 678; Plut. *Cim.* 4.6-7; Arr. *Anab.* 7.13.5. For other sources see Wycherley, *The Athenian Agora III,* 31-45; idem, "The Painted Stoa," *Phoenix* 7 (1953): 20-35; and idem, *The Stones of Athens,* 38-41; on the date see Homer A. Thompson, "Excavations in the Athenian Agora: 1949," *Hesp.* 19 (1950): 327-328. Cimon's wife was Isodice, an Alcmaeonid (Plut. *Cim.* 4.10; J. K. Davies, *Athenian Propertied Families* [Oxford: Oxford University Press,

1971], 376-378). The date of his marriage to her is under dispute; see W. R. Connor, "Two Notes on Cimon," *TAPA* 98 (1967): 67-71.

34. Ar. *Lys.* 677-679 and Schol. on *Lys.* 678; *Anecd. Bekk.*, s.v. *Gerra;* Bothmer, *Amazons,* 163. The Amazon name, *Pisianassa,* found on a bell-crater, is the feminine form of *Pisianax* and may recall the Stoa's builder. See ibid., 200.

35. Plin. *HN* 35.58. For discussion of the vases see Bothmer, *Amazons,* 161-174; and Barron, "New Light on Old Walls," 33-45.

36. Barron, "New Light on Old Walls," 39.

37. Thuc. 2.34.1. For funeral orations see H. Strasburger, "Thukydides und die politische Selbstdarstellung der Athener," *Hermes* 86 (1958): 20-24; and Kennedy, *The Art of Persuasion in Greece,* 154-166. Despite Thucydides' statement that the custom was "ancestral"—that is, one going back at least to Solon's time—the dating has been contested. See A. W. Gomme, *A Historical Commentary on Thucydides* (Oxford: Oxford University Press, 1956), 2:94-98.

38. Kennedy, *The Art of Persuasion in Greece,* 154-155.

39. Hdt. 9.27.1-5.

40. For an account of the rise of Athenian imperialism and the Peloponnesian War see Ehrenberg, *From Solon to Socrates,* 192-332.

41. Walters, "Rhetoric as Ritual," 2.

42. Ibid., 10-16.

43. For the role of the Plataeans in the battle of Marathon see Hdt. 6.108 and 111.1-2; for their role in funeral oratory see Pl. *Menex.* 240 c; Lys. 2.20-23; Isoc. 4.97; Dem. 60.10-11. On the Argive dead see Hom. *Il.* 14.114; Paus. 1.39.2. See also Walters, "Rhetoric as Ritual," 10-14.

44. Isoc. 4.68-70; also 6.42, 7.193, and 2.75.

45. Aesch. *Eum.* 685-690.

46. Dem. 60.8.

47. Lys. 2.4-6. Lysias's authorship of this speech has been challenged on stylistic grounds, but the differences from his usual style may be the result of the requirements of the genre (Walters, "Rhetoric as Ritual," 20, n. 5).

48. Adkins, *Merit and Responsibility,* 30-36 and 154-163.

49. See Chapter Six above.

50. For the subjects of these sculptures see Martin Robertson, "The Sculptures of the Parthenon," supplement to *Greece & Rome* 10 (1963): 46-60; Rhys Carpenter, *The Architects of the Parthenon* (Baltimore: Penguin Books, 1970); R. J. Hopper, *The Acropolis* (London: Weidenfeld and Nicolson, 1971); Wycherley, *The Stones of Athens,* 112-124; Frank Brommer, *The Sculptures of the Parthenon* (London: Thames and Hudson, 1979).

51. Plut. *Per.* 12.4.

52. Herington, *Athena Parthenos and Athena Polias,* 52–67; the quotations are found on 56 and 66.

53. Pind. *Pyth.* 8.15–17; Bacchyl. 15.57–63; Pl. *Rep.* 378 b–e; Apollod. *Bibl.* 1.6.1–2; Francis Vian, *La guerre des Géants* (Paris: Libraire c. Klincksieck, 1952), 287; Herington, *Athena Parthenos and Athena Polias,* 60–61.

54. Pherec. fr. 15 in Jacoby, *FGrH* I A 64, and fr. 151 and 152 in *FGrH* I A 98; Aesch. *Suppl.* 287–289 and *PV* 415–416. For Amazons in Pindar see *Ol.* 8.47 and *Nem.* 3.36–39; in tragedy, Eur. *HF* 408–418, *Hipp.* 10 and 305–309, and *Ion* 1144–1145; in comedy, Ar. *Lys.* 677–679.

55. Hellanicus fr. 16 and 17 in Jacoby, *FGrH* 3 B 45–46.

56. Harding, "Atthis and Politeia," 151.

57. Ibid., 148–160.

58. Plut. *Thes.* 27.2–7.

59. Aesch. *Eum.* 625–628.

CHAPTER 2

1. Hdt. 4.110.1. G. W. Elderkin ("Oitosyros and Oiorpata," *AJP* 56 [1935]: 342–346) supports Herodotus's contention of the Scythian origin of the Amazons with linguistic arguments.

2. Hdt. 4.110–117; and Chapters Four and Five above.

3. Diod. 17.77.1–3; Curt. 6.5.24–32; Just. *Epit.* 12.3; also Strabo 11.5.4. On the episode of the Amazon queen see W. W. Tarn, *Alexander the Great* (Cambridge: Cambridge University Press, 1948), 2:326–329.

4. Plut. *Alex.* 46.2.

5. Arr. *Anab.* 4.15.1–6.

6. J. J. Bachofen, *Das Mutterrecht: Eine Untersuchung über die Gynaikokratie der alten Welt nach ihrer religiösen und rechtlichen Natur* (Stuttgart, 1861). For a translation of selected writings by Bachofen, including an excerpt from *Das Mutterrecht,* see Ralph Manheim, trans., *Myth, Religion, and Mother Right* (Princeton: Princeton University Press, 1967). For criticism of Bachofen's thesis see Pembroke, "Women in Charge," 1–35; Bamberger, "The Myth of Matriarchy," 263–267; Elizabeth Fee, "The Sexual Politics of Victorian Social Anthropology," in *Clio's Consciousness Raised* ed. Mary S. Hartman and Lois Banner (New York: Octagon Books, 1976), 90–92; Marylin B. Arthur, "Review: Classics," *Signs* 2 (1976): 383–387.

7. Sarah Pomeroy, "A Classical Scholar's Perspective on Matriarchy," in *Liberating Women's History,* ed. Bernice A. Carroll (Urbana: University of Illinois Press, 1976), 221. Pomeroy explains the idea of the Amazon from one perspective (with which I am in agreement) as follows:

[T]he Greeks tended to view the non-Greek world as topsy-turvy and opposite from the Greek world. In most of the Greek world women were in a subordinate position. Hence evolved the symmetrical view that male/female relationships would be the opposite among the barbarians. Herodotus (e.g., IV, 26), indeed, reported that among some barbarians women actually held equal power with men. The notion of an Amazon society then would be the *reductio ad absurdum* of the distorted Greek view of the non-Greek world [Pomeroy's italics].

8. Hom. *Il.* 6.490–493. The identical norm is expressed in Telemachus's rebuke of his mother, Penelope (Hom. *Ody.* 1.356–359): "Go into your house, and see to your own tasks, the loom and the distaff, and bid your handmaidens go about their task. Song will concern men, all of them and me especially."

9. Hdt. 1.30–31.

10. Arist. *Pol.* 1259 b 2–4; Lacey, *The Family in Classical Athens*, 21–22. The methodology of Rosaldo ("Women, Culture, and Society: A Theoretical Overview," 17–42) is useful for analyzing the values of Athenian patriarchy in mythology. Although a patriarchy is characterized by the areas of male dominance cited in the text, not every patriarchy expresses that dominance with identical institutions or to the same degree of power.

11. See Wolff, "Marriage Law and Family Organization in Ancient Athens," 43–95; Lacey, *The Family in Classical Athens*, 100–176; Pomeroy, *Goddesses, Whores, Wives, and Slaves*, 57–92.

12. For illustrations see P. E. Arias, *A History of 1,000 Years of Greek Vase Painting* (New York: Harry N. Abrams, 1962), pl. 186 and 187.

13. Bothmer, *Amazons*, 143 (vase 30), 147–148, and pl. LXXI, 4. Some have seen a note of imploring in Penthesilea's eyes; however that may be, Merck ("The City's Achievements: The Patriotic Amazonomachy and Ancient Athens," 106) correctly observes that "the Penthesilea cup returns the sexual to the military episode with a vengeance."

14. See Pembroke, "Women in Charge"; Vidal-Naquet, "Esclavage et gynécocratie," 75–80; Zeitlin, "The Dynamics of Misogyny," 149–153.

15. Jane Ellen Harrison, *Themis* (Cambridge: Cambridge University Press, 1927), 261–273; Joseph Campbell, *The Masks of God: Occidental Mythology* (1964; New York: Viking, 1970), 9–17.

16. H. J. Rose (*A Handbook of Greek Mythology*, 6th ed. [New York: Dutton, 1959], 261–262) regards Cecrops's invention of marriage as "a fourth- or third-century rationalization of the legend."

17. Varro in Aug. *Civ. D.* 18.9; Pembroke, "Women in Charge," 26–27; Vidal-Naquet, "Esclavage et gynécocratie," 77–78.

18. Bamberger's conclusion concerning the message of South American myths of matriarchy ("The Myth of Matriarchy," 280) is likely applicable to the Amazon myth, although to what extent it is, is unknowable:

The myths constantly reiterate that women did not know how to
handle power when they had it. The loss is thereby justified so long as
women choose to accept the myth. The Rule of Women, instead of
heralding a promising future, harks back to a past darkened by repeated
failures.

19. I have translated each Greek work twice to bring out its full meaning.
20. Ath. 13.555 d; Schol. T. Eust. Hom. *Il.* 18.483; Schol. Ar. *Plut.* 773;
Joannis Antiochenus fr. 13.5 in Carolus Müller, *Fragmenta Historicorum
Graecorum* (1851; Frankfurt am Main, Minerva, 1975), 4:547.
21. Pl. *Rep.* 449 b–464 d.
22. Pl. *Rep.* 451 d–e.
23. Pl. *Rep.* 457 c–d.
24. Socrates perhaps came to think about women's abilities under the influence of Aspasia of Miletus, an educated and intelligent hetaera and the mis-
tress of Pericles. Socrates held the view that women were in no way inferior
to men (Xen. *Symp.* 2.9). In defense of his opinions he probably used as illustrations Aspasia's political and rhetorical acumen and the military prowess of
the Persian queen Rhodogyne, which Aeschines of Sphettus, a follower
of Socrates, later included in his dialogue *Aspasia*. See Joseph Vogt, "Von
der Gleichwertigkeit der Geschlechter in der bürgerlichen Gesellschaft der
Griechen," *Abhandlungen der Geists- und Sozialwissench. Klasse* 2 (1960):
229–230; Heinrich Dittmar, *Aischines von Sphettos* (Berlin: Weidmannsche,
1912), 46–47.
25. Winnington-Ingram, "Clytemnestra and the Vote of Athena," 132–
133.
26. Aesch. *Ag.* 40–247.
27. Aesch. *Ag.* 206–17.
28. Aesch. *Ag.* 799–806. Aeschylus does not mention the traditional pretext for Iphigenia's presence at Aulis, her marriage to Achilles (Apollod. *Epit.*
3.22), but allusions to sacrifices that precede marriage (*Ag.* 65 and 227) hint
at it. See Fraenkel, *Aeschylus: Agamemnon*, 2:40–41; Zeitlin, "The Motif of
the Corrupted Sacrifice in Aeschylus' *Oresteia*," 465. Lebeck (*The Oresteia*,
70) points out: "Each time the word [*proteleia*, preliminary sacrifice] occurs
in the *Agamemnon*, a reference to Helen is close beside it, strengthening the
suggestion of a fatal wedding." See Chapter Five, n. 23, below.
29. See Marylin Arthur, "Politics and Pomegranates: An Intepretation of
the Homeric Hymn to Demeter," *Arethusa* 10 (1977): 7–47, for a reading of
the hymn as Demeter's, and through her every woman's, "search for recognition and identity in a male-dominated cosmos" (8).
30. Aesch. *Ag.* 1625–1627; Vernant, "Hestia-Hermès," 135:

Aegisthus did not receive the scepter *aph' Hestias* [from Hestia, i.e., the hearth]; it has been passed to him by the subterfuge of a woman, herself a stranger to the hearth of the Atreidae, and, moreover, in the way of a woman: in and by the bed.

For the animal imagery see *Ag.* 1258–1259; B. Hughes Fowler, "Aeschylus' Imagery," *C&M* 28 (1967): 34–39; and Lebeck, *The Oresteia,* 50–51.

31. This scene is discussed in Chapter Five above.

32. Aesch. *Ag.* 1258–1259 and 1125–1126.

33. Aesch. *Ag.* 897–898 and 1435; Vernant, "Hestia-Hermès," 134–135.

34. For marriage and children as a woman's right see Isae. 2.7–9 and 8.36; Soph. *El.* 164–165; Lacey, *The Family in Classical Greece,* 111. When Antigone is being led off to her entombment, she laments that she had no share of marriage (Soph. *Ant.* 810–816 and 867). Aeschylus's Electra alludes to her desire for marriage (*Cho.* 486–487).

35. Aesch. *Ag.* 908–909 and 958–967. For the wife as keeper of the husband's property within the house see Chapters Three and Five above.

36. Arist. *Pol.* 1253 a 9–18; also Isoc. 15.254:

Since the power to persuade one another and to make our desires known is implanted in us, not only have we escaped living in a bestial manner but we have also come together and inhabited cities, laid down laws, discovered skills. Just about everything devised by us has been obtained by speech.

See Segal, *Tragedy and Civilization,* 55–57, for an incisive treatment of language in the *Oresteia.*

37. The Argive elders understand Cassandra's references to Thyestes' children (Aesch. *Ag.* 1106, 1200–1201, 1242) but not those to Agamemnon's impending murder (1105, 1112–1113, 1119–1120, 1245, 1251–1255, 1310), nor do they respond to her prophecy of Orestes' return (1280–1283). They accept her announcement of her own death for the purpose of questioning her submissiveness (1297–1298). *Logos* (word) and *lego* (speak) occur often in Cassandra's interchange with the Chorus (1089, 1120, 1129, 1197, 1203, 1229), underscoring the failure to communicate and marking a return to bestiality.

38. Pl. *Euthphr.* 14 c.

39. Aesch. *Ag.* 972; Zeitlin, "The Motif of the Corrupted Sacrifice in the *Oresteia,*" 480. Concerning Clytemnestra's "most horrifying parody of ritual," Zeitlin observes (473), referring to lines 1384–1387:

Agamemnon's blood is a libation, and with the three strokes she gave him, each one drenching her in blood, she makes precise allusion to the customary rite of pouring three libations after the feast—one to the Olympians, one to the Chthonians, and one to Zeus the Savior. The inversion is twofold in implication. Not only is the libation Agamemnon's blood rather than wine, but Zeus the Savior, the *agathos daimōn* [good spirit] who crowns the feast with blessings, is distorted here into Zeus of Hades, the Savior (keeper) of the dead.

40. For this view of the function of sacrifice see René Girard, *Violence and the Sacred*, trans. Patrick Gregory (Baltimore: Johns Hopkins University Press, 1977).

41. Aeschylus recaptured an archaic belief found in Homer and Hesiod that the king whose judgments were just brought about peace and prosperity for his community. See Hom. *Ody.* 19.109–114; also Hes. *Op.* 225–235, esp. 225–227:

> The community flourishes, and the people in it flower for those who give to the foreigner and citizen straight judgments and do not turn aside from the straight and narrow.

See M. L. West, *Hesiod: Works and Days* (Oxford: Oxford University Press, 1978), 213; and Charles Segal, "Nature and the World of Man in Greek Literature," *Arion* 2 (1963): 25–27 and 33–35, esp. 26:

> The evil act has a physical quality, then, which disrupts the closely compacted order of the natural and human worlds, the "topocosm," the total environment with which man and his city must stand in a life-giving relationship.

42. Aesch. *Ag.* 659–660. On this use of the imagery see John Peradotto, "Some Patterns of Nature Imagery in the *Oresteia*," *AJP* 85 (1964): 378–379.

43. Aesch. *Ag.* 1348–1392. For the sacred marriage see Aesch. fr. 66 in Nauck, *TGF* 16 (quoted in Chapter Five above); Eur. fr. 898 in *TGF* 648; Mircea Eliade, *Patterns in Comparative Religion* (1958; Cleveland: World Publishing, 1963), 75–93; M. L. West, *Hesiod: Theogony* (Oxford: Oxford University Press, 1966), 199–200: for sacred marriage in the *Agamemnon* see Richmond Y. Hathorn, *Tragedy, Myth, and Mystery* (Bloomington: Indiana University Press, 1966), 59–61.

44. Aesch. *Ag.* 1655 and 1235–1236. The translation of 1235–1236 follows Young's ("Gentler Medicines in the *Agamemnon*," 17) restoration to line 1235 of the MS reading *aran*.

CHAPTER 3

1. Hdt. 4.110–117. For these reversals see Rosellini and Saïd, "Usages de femmes et autres nomoi chez les 'sauvages' d'Hérodote," 998–1003;

Carlier-Détienne, "Les Amazones font la guerre et l'amour," 18–22; Tyrrell, "A View of the Amazons," 2–3.

2. The ship was a male realm apart from women, who entered it as passengers or captives, never as citizens. The Chorus of old men in Aristophanes' *Lysistrata* (671–675) reflects this exclusiveness when it expresses the fear that the slightest concession to the women will lead to their building ships and confronting the men in a sea battle. Ships belong to men, and by saying that Amazons cannot sail, Herodotus is saying that they are not men.

3. Vidal-Naquet, "Esclavage et gynécocratie," 77–78; Segal, *Tragedy and Civilization*, 35–38; and Chapter Two above, *passim*.

4. Lacey, *The Family in Classical Greece*, 109.

5. Diod. 3.52.3 and 3.66.5–6.

6. Diod. 4.48.5.

7. G. L. Barber, *The Historian Ephorus* (Cambridge: Cambridge University Press, 1935), 112–123.

8. Strabo 11.5.3.

9. Strabo (1.2.7–9) is commenting upon Homer's use of myths and he quotes from *Odyssey* 6.232. "Monstrous" is used etymologically as something that serves to warn; "portentous" would also translate the Greek.

10. Merck ("The City's Achievements," 113) also contends that "the construction of the Amazon myth cannot be separated from a context of patriarchal dominance," but she does not approach the myth from the viewpoint of reversals. DuBois (*Centaurs and Amazons,* 25–40) emphasizes the data of the Amazon myth as stressing difference, not reversal, from the patriarchy. The hostility of the Amazons to marriage brings about "*polemos,* war between differing kinds, between the Greek male human being and his bestial, barbarian, female enemies" (150).

11. Men. fr. 546. For background to these reversals see Rosaldo, "Women, Culture, and Society," 17–42, who documents aspects of "a universal asymmetry in cultural evaluations of the sexes." For the Greek polarity of inside/outside see Vernant, "Hestia-Hermès," 125–132.

12. The woman was kept close to home by her motherly and wifely duties, for reasons of her own protection, and by the need to keep her chastity above reproach. See Xen. *Oec.* 7 (quoted in part in n. 14 below); Lacey, *The Family in Classical Greece*, 158–162 and 167–169; Pomeroy, *Goddesses, Whores, Wives, and Slaves*, 71–73. In Aristophanes' *Lysistrata*, a comedy about marriage, Calonice complains (16–19): "Getting out is hard for women. Fuss over the husband. Wake up the slave. Put the baby to bed, wash and feed him."

13. Xen. *Oec.* 7.18–25. Cf. Electra addressing her husband (Eur. *El.* 73–76):

You have enough to do with the outdoor work. I must see to the indoor work. It is a pleasure for a working man, when he comes in from the outside, to find everything in order.

14. Xen. *Oec.* 7.30:

The law which yokes man and woman together also praises these arrangements. Just as the god made them partners in children, so also the law establishes that those arrangements, which the god implanted in each to be capable of doing, are good.

15. Diod. 2.45.1–3 and 3.53.1–3; Strabo 11.5.1.

16. Webster, *Potter and Patron in Classical Athens*, 241–242; see also 226–228.

17. Amazons are indoors at Theseus's wedding feast with Phaedra (Apollod. *Epit.* 1.17), but a different impetus to mythmaking is operating. See Chapter Five above.

18. Hipp. *Aër.* 17; Hellanicus fr. 16 in Jacoby, *FGrH* 3 B 45; Apollod. *Bibl.* 2.5.9; Diod. 2.45.3; Strabo 11.5.1; Arr. *Anab.* 7.13.2; Just. *Epit.* 2.4; Curt. 6.5.28; Schol. and Eust. on Hom. *Il.* 3.189. Philostratus (*Her.* 216–217) derived the name from their not being nourished at the breast. Dionysius Scytobrachion outdid the tradition by having both breasts cauterized (Diod. 3.53.3.).

19. For example, Hecuba to Hector (Hom. *Il.* 22.83) and Clytemnestra to Orestes (Aesch. *Cho.* 896–898).

20. That is, they are armed with the spear and shield or bow. The battle-ax is rare on black-figure vases (Boardman, *Athenian Black Figure Vases*, 231).

21. F. E. Adcock, *The Greek and Macedonian Art of War* (Berkeley and Los Angeles: University of California Press, 1957), 4; Anderson, *Military Theory and Practice in the Age of Xenophon*, 13–15.

22. Tyrtaeus fr. 10; also Eur. *HF* 190–192; Ar. *Vesp.* 1081–1083; Pl. *La.* 109 e.

23. Arist. *Pol.* 1253 a 19–21: "The *polis* is prior in nature to the household and to each of us, for the whole must be prior to the part." See also 1253 a 21–29.

24. Hdt. 7.9; Polybius (13.3.4) noted that the ancients did not use "unseen shafts hurled from afar against one another, but only fighting that took place hand-to-hand at close quarters did they consider decisive."

25. Pind. *Ol.* 8.46–47; *Nem.* 3.38; Aesch. *Supp.* 288; Xen. *Anab.* 4.4.16; Callim. *Dian.* 241; Strabo 11.5.1; Plut. *Quaest. Graec.* 6.5.26 and 28; Quint. Smyrn. 1.597. Penthesilea, however, fights in hoplite armor (Quint. Smyrn. 1.142–151). For an illustration of both types of weaponry see Bothmer, *Amazons*, pl. LXXXV, a.

26. Hom. *Il.* 4.242 and 11.384–395; Soph. *Aj.* 1120–1122; Eur. *HF* 188–203. Even so, if Agamemnon had to fall at a woman's hands, Apollo grieves that it was not by "the rushing, far-darting bows" of Amazons (Aesch. *Eum.* 627–628). See also Aesch. *Supp.* 287–289: "If you were carrying bows, I would have likened you to husbandless, flesh-eating Amazons."

27. A. S. F. Gow, "Notes on the *Persae* of Aeschylus," *JHS* 48 (1928): 156; Anderson, *Military Theory and Practice in the Age of Xenophon,* 115–116.

28. Semonides 7.57–70; Arist. *Pol.* 1289 b 27–41; 1297 b 16–18, and 1321 a 13–15; Pind. *Ol.* 8.46–47; Eur. *Hipp.* 581–582. Strepsiades laments the debts run up by his son, who "keeps his hair long, rides horses, and drives his team, even in his dreams" (Ar. *Nub.* 14–16).

29. Hdt. 7.135.3, 7.64.2, 4.5, and 4.70; Rosellini and Saïd, "Usages de femmes et autres nomoi chez les 'sauvages' d'Hérodote," 971, n. 119.

30. Aesch. *Cho.* 889. Clytemnestra, in fact, killed Agamemnon with a robe and sword, not an ax (*Ag.* 1382–1387).

31. At Thermopylae the Persians had to be whipped into battle (Hdt. 7.223.3). See also Hipp. *Aër.* 16.

32. Hdt. 7.41.

33. Isae. 3.18–27. Wives at marriage, and children on the tenth day after birth, were enrolled with the father's phratry, a social group of obscure origin. Its lists were challengeable in court. Another organization, the deme, in which citizens were registered according to geographical location as opposed to kinship in the phratry, became more important for registration in the fifth century. See Isae. 3.75, 3.79, and 8.18–19; Dem. 59.122 and 57.54; Lacey, *The Family in Classical Greece,* 96–97 and 111–112. The Greeks distrusted papers, and although documentation and litigation were increasing throughout the classical period, they would disregard written evidence in the face of persuasive argumentation.

34. On mastery, or guardianship (*kyrieia*), and the passive role of women in negotiating their first marriage see Wolff, "Marriage Law and Family Organization in Ancient Athens," 46–65; A. R. W. Harrison, *The Law of Athens* (Oxford: Oxford University Press, 1968), 1:5–12, 19–21, and 74. On marriage in general see Lacey, *The Family in Classical Greece,* 105–112; and Pomeroy, *Goddesses, Whores, Wives, and Slaves,* 62–65.

35. Plut. *Mor.* 12.9, 10, 11, 14, 16, 19, 26, 28, and 32.

36. Diod. 2.45.2.

37. Plut. *Thes.* 26.2; Hdt. 4.113.2; Dio Chrys. 8.32; Quint. Smyrn. 1.671–674. The discrepancy between their man-loving and man-hating ways is discussed in Chapter Four above.

38. Strabo 11.5.1.

39. Lacey, *The Family in Classical Greece,* 113 and 147–148.

142 · Notes to Pages 55–63

40. Xen. *Lac. Pol.* 1.3–4; Pomeroy, *Goddesses, Whores, Wives, and Slaves,* 62–63 and 74.

41. Strabo 11.5.1; Diod. 2.45.3; Just. *Epit.* 2.4.

42. Strabo 11.5.1.

43. Bennett, *Religious Cults Associated with Amazons,* 73.

44. For a discussion of Amazon religion see Chapter Four above.

45. Hom. *Il.* 6.172–186, 3.181–189, and 2.811–814; Arctinus, *Aethiopis,* in Proclus, *Chrestomathia* 175–180; Pherec. fr. 15 in Jacoby, *FGrH* I A 64; Hdt. 4.110; Lys. 2.4; Apollod. *Bibl.* 2.5.9; Diod. 2.45.1, 3.52.1, and 3.53.1; Strabo 12.3.5; Just. *Epit.* 2.4; Paus. 3.25.3 and 7.2.7; Steph. Byz., s.v. *Amazones* (following Ephorus); Aesch. *PV* 415–419 and 723–727.

46. Diod. 3.53.1.

47. Hom. *Il.* 1.268; Eur. *IA* 705; Hes. *Th.* 274–275; Apollod. *Bibl.* 2.5.11; Aesch. *Supp.* 284–286; Diod. 3.53.4–6; Hom. *Ody.* 1.1–4, 1.22–24, and 9.68; Segal, "The Raw and the Cooked in Greek Literature," 291–293.

48. Rosellini and Saïd, "Usages de femmes et autres nomoi chez les 'sauvages' d'Hérodote," 955–971; Hdt. 3.17–22.

49. Diod. 3.52.4 and 3.54.1.

50. Diod. 3.53.4; Helen Diner, *Mothers and Amazons: The First Feminine History of Culture* (1930; New York: Julian Press, 1965), 133: "Amazons . . . practiced animal husbandry but no agriculture . . ."; Donald J. Sobol, *The Amazons of Greek Mythology* (New York: A. S. Barnes, 1972), 20: "The staples of life came so easily that farming had not yet been discovered."

51. Strabo 11.5.1; Hes. *Op.* 117–119; Hom. *Ody.* 9.106–11, 116–124, and 189; Pierre Vidal-Naquet, "Valeurs religieuses et mythiques de la terre et du sacrifice dans l'Odyssée," in *Problèmes de la terre en Grèce,* ed. M. I. Finley (Paris: Mouton, 1973), 278–280.

52. Moschion fr. 6.3–15 in Nauck, *TGF* 813–814.

53. Diod. 3.49.3.

54. Hdt. 4.142 and 6.11–12; cf. Thuc. 5.91 and 6.77.1.

55. Hipp. *Aër.* 16.

56. Arist. *Pol.* 1327 b 18–34.

57. Hdt. 9.122.3; Hipp. *Aër.* 24.

58. Steph. Byz., s.v. *Amazones.*

59. Arist. *HA* 608 a 22–28 and 608 a 33–b 4; Pl. *Rep.* 398–399 and 410 b–411 (for the opposition of *hēmeros/agrios* in the training of warrior auxiliaries); Thuc. 2.40.1; Segal, "The Raw and the Cooked in Greek Literature," 296–298.

60. Alvin W. Gouldner, *Enter Plato* (New York: Basic Books, 1965), 27.

61. Thuc. 2.39.

62. Aesch. *Ag.* 914–974. Agamemnon sees himself as being softened (918–919), and the interchange as a battle (940) and a contest (942).

CHAPTER 4

1. Jean-Pierre Vernant, "La guerre des cités," in *Mythe et société en grèce ancienne* (Paris: François Maspero, 1974), 37–38. See also duBois, *Centaurs and Amazons,* 69–71; and idem, "On Horse/Men, Amazons, and Endogamy," 45: "The Amazon represents a pre-adolescent female/male being, whose transvestism and male attributes complemented her worship of the huntress Artemis."

2. The Amazons are but one permutation among others whose makeup is on the margin of the twofold imperative mentioned above.

3. Leach, *Culture and Communication,* 77–79. See also Victor Turner, "Myth and Symbol," in *International Encyclopedia of the Social Sciences* (New York: Macmillan, 1967), 576–582; and idem, *Dramas, Fields, and Metaphors* (Ithaca, N.Y.: Cornell University Press, 1974), 231–271.

4. Plut. *Thes.* 27.7; Deubner, *Attische Feste,* 225.

5. Plut. *Thes.* 23.5; Parke, *Festivals of the Athenians,* 75–79.

6. Plut. *Thes.* 4 and 17.7.

7. Hes. *Op.* 383–384: "At the setting of the Pleiades, daughters of Atlas, begin . . . the plowing" (late October).

8. The ancient evidence has been collected by Jacoby, *FGrH* 3 b 288–289. See also Philochorus fr 15 and 16 in *FGrH* 3 B 102; Deubner, *Attische Feste,* 142–146; Ferguson, "The Salaminoi of Heptaphylai and Sounion," 1–74; Henri Jeanmaire, *Couroi et Courètes* (Lille: Bibliothèque universitaire, 1939), 338–358; Nilsson, *Cults, Myths, Oracles, and Politics in Ancient Greece,* 28–36; Delcourt, *Hermaphrodite,* 15–17; Parke, *Festivals of the Athenians,* 77–81.

9. Paus. 1.2.1; [Pl.] *Ax.* 365a; Plut. *Thes.* 27.6; Judeich, *Topographie von Athen,* 140–142; Jacoby, *FGrH* 3 b II 344–345 n. 21.

10. For the Apaturia see Deubner, *Attische Feste,* 232–234; Nilsson, *Cults, Myths, Oracles, and Politics in Ancient Greece,* 167–170; Parke, *Festivals of the Athenians,* 88–92.

11. Isae. 8.19; Andoc. 1.127; Lacey, *The Family in Classical Greece,* 26–27. Before Pericles' law on citizenship (451 B.C.) the father would have sworn only that the candidate was his son. One phratry, for which epigraphic evidence exists, required a year's removal or latency from society between clipping of the hair and voting for acceptance. See Vidal-Naquet, "Le chasseur noir et l'origine de l'éphébie athénienne," 179.

12. Harrison, *Prolegomena to the Study of Greek Religion,* 120–131; Deubner, *Attische Feste,* 50–60; Parke, *Festivals of the Athenians,* 82–88; Detienne, *The Gardens of Adonis,* 78–81.

13. C. G. Jung and C. Kerényi, *Essays on a Science of Mythology,* trans. R. F. C. Hull (1949; Princeton: Princeton University Press, 1969), 162.

14. O. W. Reinmuth, "The Genesis of the Athenian Ephebia," *TAPA* 83 (1952): 34–50; Chrysis Pélékidis, *Histoire de l'éphebie attique des origines à 31 avant Jésus-Christ* (Paris: E. de Boccard, 1962), 71–79; Vidal-Naquet, "Le chasseur noir et l'origine de l'éphébie athénienne," 176; Arist. *Pol.* 42.

15. This is shown by line 12 of an inscription (363/62 B.C.) recording the settlement of a dispute among the Salaminian families over the management of the Oschophoria. See Ferguson, "The Salaminioi of Heptaphylai and Sounion," 20–21; Franciszek Sokolowski, *Lois sacrées des cités grecques,* suppl. (Paris: E. de Boccard, 1962), 49.

16. See Vidal-Naquet, "Le chasseur noir et l'origine de l'éphébie athénienne"; and idem, "Les jeunes: Le cru, l'infant grec et le cuit," 145–162.

17. Ael. *VH* 13.1; for these festivals see Deubner, *Attische Feste,* 9–17 and 207–208; Parke, *Festivals of the Athenians,* 139–143.

18. Ar. *Lys.* 645; the reading of *katacheousa* in MS R as "shedding" is supported by ceramic evidence. See L. B. Ghali-Kahil, "Autour de l'Artémis attique," *Antike Kunst* 8 (1965): 20–33; and Christiane Sourvinou, "Aristophanes, *Lysistrata, 641–647,*" CQ 21 (1971): 339–342.

19. The following description of the marriage ceremony is drawn mainly from M. Collignon, "Cérémonies du mariage," in *Dictionnaire des antiquités grecques et romaines,* ed. C. Daremberg and Edmond Saglio (Paris: Librairie Hachette, 1918), III, 2, 1647–1654.

20. W. Paton, *The Greek Anthology* (London: William Heinemann, 1927), 1:448.

21. Plut. *Mor.* 12.36; Soph. fr. 524 in Nauck, *TGF* 257–258.

22. Lys. 1.6.

23. J. K. Campbell, *Honour, Family, and Patronage* (Oxford: Oxford University Press, 1964), 58; Lacey, *The Family in Classical Greece,* 107 and 110–111.

24. Hom. *Il.* 3.189 with Scholiast, who glosses *antianeira* as "those equal to or opposing men."

25. Proclus, *Chrestomathia* 175–180.

26. Quint. Smyrn. 1.48–61 and 659–674.

27. Hom. *Ody.* 6.101–109.

28. Apollod. *Bibl.* 3.12.4, 1.9.4, and 1.4.4–5; Hom. *Ody.* 15.250–251.

29. Hom. *Il.* 3.397; *Homeric Hymns* 5.21–30.

30. Hom. *Il.* 11.243 and 5.428–430; also Hes. *Op.* 65–66 and 73–75; Plut. *Mor.* 47.5: "The yielding of the woman to the man . . . was called grace among the ancients." Vernant, "Hestia-Hermès," 131; Paul Friedrich, *The Meaning of Aphrodite* (Chicago: University of Chicago Press, 1978), 106–107.

31. See Vernant in Detienne, *The Gardens of Adonis,* vi–vii and xxii; and Detienne, ibid., 60–122. In the second Homeric hymn to Aprhodite (6.16–

17), when Aphrodite is first introduced to the gods, "each one prayed that she would be his wedded wife and be led home to his house."

32. Farnell, *The Cults of the Greek States,* 2:620.

33. Ibid., 2:654; Martin P. Nilsson, *Geschichte der griechischen Religion* (Munich: C. H. Beck'sche, 1955), 521 n. 5; Bennett, *Religious Cults Associated with Amazons,* 61–62; Pherec. fr. 15 in Jacoby, *FGrH* I A 64; Hom. *Il.* 21.416–417 and *Ody.* 8.266–320. Aphrodite and Ares were patron gods of Thebes. Ares was worshiped from earliest times at Athens, as shown by his marriage to Aglauros, daughter of Cecrops and a figure from the earliest stratum of Athenian religion, by the name of the hill Areopagus (Hill of Ares), and by Ares' trial there for homicide (Apollod. *Bibl.* 3.14.2).

34. Hom. *Il.* 5.757–766 and 889–898, where Zeus is said to tolerate Ares' destructive ways because Ares is his son; Walter F. Otto, *The Homeric Gods,* trans. Moses Hadas (1954; Boston: Beacon, 1964); Vian, "La fonction guerrière dans la mythologie grecque," 54–57.

35. Ephorus in Schol. Ap. Rhod. 2.967 and in Steph. Bzy., s. v. *Amazones;* Just. *Epit.* 2.4.

36. Plut. *Thes.* 28.1, quoted in Chapter One above.

37. Apollod. *Epit.* 1.21; Plut. *Thes.* 30.3.

38. DuBois, "On Horse/Men, Amazons, and Endogamy," 43–44.

39. Ar. *Lys.* 785–795.

40. Apollod. *Bibl.* 3.14.4.

41. Theog. 1283–1294; Apollod. *Bibl.* 3.9.2.

42. Vidal-Naquet, "Le chasseur noir et l'origine de l'éphébie athénienne"; Detienne, *The Gardens of Adonis;* idem, *Dionysus Slain,* trans. Mireille Muellner and Leonard Muellner (Baltimore: Johns Hopkins University Press, 1979).

43. Nonnus, *Dion.* 15 and 16.

44. Eur. *Hipp;* Apollod. *Epit.* 1.17–19; Barrett, *Euripides: Hippolytus,* 1–9; Herter, "Theseus und Hippolytos," 273–292.

45. Because he received a cult, Hippolytus was likely a hero, a human whose life continued after death and who could be propitiated at his gravesite; Barrett, *Euripides: Hippolytus,* 3–6.

46. Eur. *Hipp.* 15–19 and 84–86.

47. Ap. Rhod. 2.1172–1177; Diod. 2.46.1 and 3.55.8–9; Pindar in Paus. 7.2.7; Callim. *Dian.* 237–247; Paus. 4.31.8; Hyg. *Fab.* 237. According to Pausanias (3.25.3), Amazons are also said to worship Artemis Astrateia and Apollo Amazonius at Pyrrhichus. Bennett (*Religious Cults Associated with Amazons,* 75) has tried to show from an examination of their cults that Amazons are "reflexes of the Woman they ["people who built up the pre-historic civilisation of the Aegean"] worshipped." I take the opposing stand—namely, that their worship is a reflex of their nature.

48. See Farnell, *The Cults of the Greek States*, 2:473–482; Hdt. 3.48–49 and 8.105; Arist. *Pol.* 1311 b 21–24; Soph. fr. 563 in Nauck, *TGF* 267.

49. Philostr. *VA* 4.21.

50. For Dionysus see W. K. Guthrie, *The Greeks and Their Gods* (1950; Boston: Beacon, 1955), 145–182; and E. R. Dodds, *Euripides: Bacchae*, 2nd ed. (Oxford: Oxford University Press, 1960), xi–xxv. For Dionysus's effeminacy and cowardice see, for example, Aristophanes' *Frogs*.

51. Eur. *Bacch.* 820–830; and Charles Segal, "The Menace of Dionysus: Sex Roles and Reversals in Euripides' *Bacchae*," *Arethusa* 11 (1978): 185–202.

CHAPTER 5

1. Eur. *Hipp.* 618–624; Apollod. *Bibl.* 1.3.6 and 3.4.3; *Homeric Hymns* 3.323; Hes. *Th.* 927–929; Aesch. *Eum.* 658–661 with *tou keklēmenou*, following Thompson, *The Oresteia of Aeschylus*, 2:217.

2. For androgyny in Greek mythology and cults see Delcourt, *Hermaphrodite*, 5–50.

3. Apollod. *Bibl.* 2.3; Hom. *Il.* 6.152–159.

4. Pind. *Ol.* 13.91, with Scholia to line 130; Plut. *Mor.* 17.248.

5. Apollod. *Bibl.* 2.5.9. In antiquity the myth received much elaboration with regard to Heracles' companions, his method of obtaining the girdle, and the time of the labor (before or after the Trojan War). For these problems see Robert, *Heldensage*, 2:462–465 and 558–561.

6. Liddell and Scott, *A Greek-English Lexicon*, 760, s.v. *zōstēr*; Hom. *Ody.* 11.245.

7. Plut. *Thes.* 26.1; Pind. fr. 175; Robert, *Heldensage*, 2:730–732; Jacoby, *FGrH* 3 b 437–440; Herter, "Theseus," 1149–1153. According to Hegias of Troizen, Antiope fell in love with Theseus and betrayed the Amazons' fortress to Heracles (Paus. 1.2.1).

8. Hellanicus fr. 20 in Jacoby, *FGrH* 3 B 46; Plut. *Thes.* 31–34; Robert, *Heldensage*, 2:731.

9. For these vases see Bothmer, *Amazons*, 124–130.

10. The most popular name for the son is *Hippolytus*; Pindar (fr. 176) gives *Demophon*, which is likely the older Attic tradition. Hippolytus was probably imported into the myth from Troizen on account of his name (cf. *Hippolyte*), his virginity, and his hunting prowess. See Robert, *Heldensage*, 2:733.

11. Paus. 1.2.1; Diod. 4.28.3–4; Plut. *Thes.* 27.6.

12. Men of the lower middle-class and the upper classes considered it disgraceful for their women to work outside the house. When descended upon by fourteen female relatives, Aristarchus was at a loss until Socrates suggested

that they support themselves by weaving (Xen. *Mem.* 2.7.2–12; Lacey, *The Family in Classical Greece,* 170–171).

13. Aesch. *Ag.* 1232–1236, with Young's ("Gentler Medicines in the *Agamemnon,*" 17) restoration of *aran* to line 1235; Froma I. Zeitlin, "Postscript to Sacrificial Imagery in the *Oresteia (Ag.* 1235–37)," *TAPA* 97 (1966): 650–651.

14. Aesch. *Ag.* 1380–1392.

15. Aesch. *Cho.* 1011; *Ag.* 1435–1436.

16. Hom. *Il.* 22.442–446. Odysseus is first recognized at Ithaca by Eurycleia, who bathes his feet (Hom. *Ody.* 19.392–393 and 467–475).

17. Aesch. *Ag.* 1107–1109 and 1126–1129.

18. For Helen the weaver see Kenneth John Atchity, "Structure in *Iliad* 3," *Classical Bulletin* 54 (1977): 74–75. On weaving as a motif for spinning the lives of men and, negatively, as an encircling, entangling net see Neumann, *The Great Mother,* 226–233.

19. Hom. *Ody.* 6.182–185:

Nothing is stronger and better than that a man and a woman hold a
house in like-mindedness of thoughts. Many are the pains to their enemies, many the joys to their friends.

Solon fr. 13.5: "Grant that I be sweet to friends, bitter to enemies." For criticism of this morality see Pl. *Rep.* 331 e–336 a.

20. Aesch. *Ag.* 608 and 1228. The first space (the anceps) of the third metron of line 608 is long and terminates a word, a situation avoided in tragic iambic trimeter. That correspondence of long syllable and word ending isolates the rest of the line, allowing its hidden meaning. See James W. Halporn, Martin Ostwald, and Thomas G. Rosenmeyer, *The Meters of Greek and Latin Poetry* (Indianapolis: Bobbs-Merrill, 1963), 9 and 13.

21. Aesch. *Ag.* 810–974. See, in particular, Winnington-Ingram, "Clytemnestra and the Vote of Athena," 132–134; Fraenkel, *Aeschylus: Agamemnon,* 2:371–442; Robert F. Goheen, "Aspects of Dramatic Symbolism: Three Studies in the *Oresteia,*" *AJP* 76 (1955): 115–132; Lebeck, *The Oresteia,* 74–79; Taplin, *The Stagecraft of Aeschylus,* 302–316; idem, *Greek Tragedy in Action,* 78–83.

22. Aesch. *Ag.* 1447. Clytemnestra calls the dead Agamemnon "the gladdener of the Chryseids under Ilios" (1439). "Golden girls" is Lattimore's (*Aeschylus I: Oresteia,* 82) inspired translation. Clytemnestra is referring to Agamemnon's dalliances at Troy; for her sexual jealousy see Winnington-Ingram, "Clytemnestra and the Vote of Athena," 135–136.

23. Odysseus escorted Iphigenia to Aulis, where she was to marry Achilles (Apollod. *Epit.* 3.22). Although Aeschylus does not mention the incident,

and we must beware of introducing extradramatic myths into the narrative, the reference to Odysseus at this point is too appropriate to be accidental and it is supported by the imagery. See Chapter Two, note 28, above.

24. Aesch. *Ag.* 895–913.

25. Aesch. *Ag.* 231–247; Hugh Lloyd-Jones, "The Robes of Iphigeneia," *CR* 2 (1952): 132–135; Lebeck, *The Oresteia*, 80–86.

26. Aesch. *Ag.* 1228; see note 49 of this chapter for a translation.

27. As Clytemnestra's sacrificial victim, Agamemnon had to be perfect and without blemish (she calls him an *anēr teleios* [972], an "unblemished man"), and, as required in animal sacrifice, he must approach the altar "willingly," that is, without balking or crying out (Ael. *NA* 10.50; Apollon. *Mir.* 13; Plut. *Pel.* 21). For the same submission in human sacrifice see Neanthes fr. 16 in Jacoby, *FGrH* II A 195; Thompson, *The Oresteia of Aeschylus*, 2:78; Walter Burkert, "Greek Tragedy and Sacrificial Ritual," *GRBS* 7 (1966): 107. Cf. *Ag.* 1297, where the Chorus asks Cassandra if she is going to walk toward the altar "like a god-driven ox."

28. Aesch. *Ag.* 935–945.

29. Denniston and Page, *Aeschylus: Agamemnon*, 148.

30. Aesch. *Ag.* 369–384 and 750–781; *Cho.* 639–645; Lebeck, *The Oresteia*, 38–39.

31. Aesch. *Ag.* 1415–1418.

32. Aesch. *Cho.* 67 and 400–404; also *Ag.* 1019–1021.

33. Aesch. *Ag.* 1055; Young, "Gentler Medicines in the *Agamemnon*," 15.

34. Quint. 10.1.66.

35. Aesch. *Ag.* 351. *Histotribēs* (literally, "rubbing an upright thing") is emended to *isotribēs* ("wearing out equally [with Agamemnon] the ship's benches"). See Young, "Gentler Medicines in the *Agamemnon*," 15; George L. Koniaris, "An Obscene Word in Aeschylus (I)," *AJP* 101 (1980): 42–44; Wm. Blake Tyrrell, "An Obscene Word in Aeschylus (II)," ibid., 44–46.

36. See Vernant, "Hestia-Hermès," 132–138.

37. Aesch. *Ag.* 1625–1626.

38. Aesch. *Ag.* 958–974.

39. Aesch. *Cho.* 204, 236, and 503.

40. Aesch. *Ag.* 1224.

41. I owe this observation to Professor Richard W. Minadeo, of Wayne State University.

42. Aesch. *Ag.* 1389–1392.

43. Aesch. fr. 44 in Nauck *TGF* 16.

44. Aesch. *Ag.* 1235.

45. Aesch. *Cho.* 748–750 and 986–987; Zeitlin, "The Dynamics of Misogyny," 157–158.

46. Aesch. *Cho.* 585–638; Winnington-Ingram, "Clytemnestra and the

Vote of Athena," 138 n. 76; Anne Lebeck, "The First Stasimon of Aeschylus' *Choephori:* Myth and Mirror Image," *CP* 57 (1967): 182–185; Brian Vickers, *Towards Greek Tragedy,* 400–403.

47. Cf. Orestes' farewell to Athens: "May you put an inescapable wrestling hold on your enemies, one of salvation and victory of the spear" (*Eum.* 776–777).

48. Aesch. *Cho.* 991–996.

49. Aesch. *Ag.* 1223–1232:

> I say that someone is planning revenge, a strengthless lion rolling in the bed, a stay-at-home savage to my master come back. Yes, my master, for I must bear slavery's yoke. The leader of the ships and destroyer of Ilium does not know what sort is the tongue of the hateful bitch. Cheerfully, she will speak, draw out her plea, and hit the mark of secret ruin in disastrous outcome. She dares such things: the female is the murderer of the male.

50. Thuc. 7.21.3–4.

51. Adkins, *Merit and Responsibility,* 31–57 and 156–168. Apollo, in the trial scene on the Areopagus, asserts the principle that the noble man's life is more valuable than a woman's (Aesch. *Eum.* 625–626). See Grace Harris, "Furies, Witches, and Mothers," in *The Character of Kinship,* ed. Jack Goody (Cambridge: Cambridge University Press, 1973), 151:

> Agamemnon receives no blame [in the *Libation Bearers*] for Iphegenia's [*sic*] death, but no pardon either. Agamemnon as an individual and father-as-kinsman receives no mournful word or even any mention. His social personality undergoes idealization by impoverishment, its other aspects swallowed up by his jural-political status.

52. Soph. *Trach.* 582–587.

53. Aesch. *Cho.* 827–837.

54. Apollod. *Bibl.* 2.4.1–5; the Scholiast on Ap. Rhod. 4.1091 and 1515, who agrees closely with Apollodorus, cites Pherecydes as his source. See Jacoby, *FGrH* I A 61–63. There is no depiction of the shield used as a mirror dating to the fifth century B.C. or earlier, so this detail is probably a later addition. Edward Phinney, Jr. ("Perseus' Battle with the Gorgons," *TAPA* 102 [1971]: 459), concludes that the insertion of the mirror into Pherecydes' text was the work of "a Byzantine copyist who wanted to 'complete' the version of Pherecydes by fleshing it out with details from versions such as that of Lucian."

55. Apollod. *Bibl.* 2.4.2.

56. Hom. *Il.* 8.349, 9.36–37, and 14.319–320. Cf. Aesch. *PV* 792–800 (Prometheus is telling Io about her wanderings):

Cross the roaring sea until you come to the Gorgonian plains of Kisthene, where the daughters of Phorcys live, the three aged swan-shaped maidens who have a common eye and one tooth. Neither the sun with its rays looks upon them nor the moon in the night. Nearby these are the three winged sisters, the Gorgons, with hair of serpents, hateful to men, whose *effluences* no mortal *will endure looking upon* [italics added].

The italicized words are usually translated "will keep his life's breath." Harrison (*Prolegomena to the Study of Greek Religion,* 193–194) points out that the gorgons likely killed by the evil eye. The Chorus refers to this specifically when it directs Orestes to look at Aegisthus. The literature on the gorgons is extensive; see A. Furtwängler, in Roscher, *Lex.* I 1695–1727, s.v. *Gorgones und Gorgo;* Harrison, *Prolegomena to the Study of Greek Religion,* 187–197; Jocelyn M. Woodward, *Perseus: A Study in Greek Art and Legend* (Cambridge: Cambridge University Press, 1937); Howe, "The Origin and Function of the Gorgon-Head," 209–221; Feldman, "Gorgo and the Origins of Fear," 484–494.

57. Furtwängler, in Roscher, *Lex.* I 1697–1698; Howe, "The Origin and Function of the Gorgon-Head," 216.

58. Neumann, *The Great Mother,* 169–170; E. Servadio, "Note sur la tête de la Médusa," *Psyché* 3 (1948): 73–75.

59. Sándor Ferenczi, "The Symbolism of the Head of Medusa," in *Further Contributions to the Theory and Technique of Psycho-Analysis,* 2nd ed. (London: Hogarth and the Institute of Psycho-Analysis, 1950), 360; S. Freud, "Medusa's Head," in *Standard Edition of the Complete Psychological Works of Sigmund Freud* (London: Hogarth and the Institute of Psycho-Analysis, 1955), 18:273–274. Ferenczi's note was published in 1923, and Freud's in 1940, but Freud's article is dated 1922. See also Slater, *The Glory of Hera,* 17–20 and 308–333; the quotations are found on pages 18 and 330. Although I disagree with Slater's interpretation, I have learned much from his analysis of the Perseus myth. For a review of theories of the Medusa figure see Arthur A. Miller, "An Interpretation of the Symbolism of the Medusa," *American Imago* 15 (1958): 389–399; and John Glenn, "Psychoanalytic Writings on Classical Mythology and Religion: 1909–1960," *Classical World* 70 (1976–1977): 228–230.

60. See, for example, Lord Raglan, *The Hero: A Study in Tradition, Myth, and Drama* (1936; New York: Random House, 1956).

61. Furtwängler (in Roscher, *Lex.* I 1721–1727, s.v. *Gorgonen und Gorgo*) distinguishes two types: "calmy beautiful," which appeared toward the end of the fifth century B.C., and "the pathetic type," which belongs to the third century B.C.

62. Aesch. *Cho.* 543–550.

63. Aesch. *Cho.* 928–929. Gilbert Murray (*Aeschyli Septem Quae Supersunt Tragoediae* [Oxford: Oxford University Press, 1955] gives line 929 to Orestes; I follow Denys Page, *Aeschyli septem quae supersunt tragoedias* [*sic*] (Oxford: Oxford University Press, 1972).

64. Whallon, "The Serpent at the Breast," 273.

65. Aesch. *Eum.* 264–265. Cf. *Eum.* 137–139, quoted in Chapter Six, note 17, below.

66. Whallon, "The Serpent at the Breast," 274.

67. Aesch. *Eum.* 47–48 and 410–414.

68. Hom. *Ody.* 1.435; at *Ody.* 19.354–355 Eurycleia is said to have nursed Odysseus. William Whallon (*Problem and Spectacle: Studies in the Oresteia* [Heidelberg: Carl Winter, 1980], 136) suggests, on the basis of the similarity of vocabulary, that Clytemnestra is plagiarizing Hecuba's appeal to her son, Hector (*Hom. Il.* 22.82–83), a deceit that an audience familiar with Homer would perceive.

69. Aesch. *Cho.* 899–902. Aeschylus's use of silent figures was sufficiently striking to be included in Aristophanes' contest between Euripides and Aeschylus in the *Frogs* (911–927).

CHAPTER 6

1. Dem. 60.4–8; also Hdt. 7.161.3; Pl. *Menex.* 237 b–d; Isoc. 4.24 and 12.124; Hyperides 6.7; Schroeder, *De laudibus Athenarum*, 8–9.

2. Pl. *Menex.* 238 b.

3. Lys. 2.17.

4. Thuc. 2.36.1–4.

5. Pl. *Menex.* 254 c–d.

6. Pl. *Menex.* 235 b–c; Walters, "Rhetoric as Ritual," 16–18.

7. Hom. *Ody.* 4.563–569; Hes. *Op.* 168–173.

8. Hom. *Il.* 2.547–548; Schroeder, *De laudibus Athenarum*, 8–9.

9. Aesch. *Eum.* 902–913.

10. Liddell and Scott, *A Greek-English Lexicon*, 1639, s.v. *stergo*.

11. Quoted in Chapter Five above.

12. A possible justification is the jurors' faithfulness to their oath (Aesch. *Eum.* 710), or the fact that they are the best of Athena's citizens (*Eum.* 487 and Verrall, *The 'Eumenides' of Aeschylus,* 170). Lattimore (*Aeschylus I: Oresteia* 167), evidently sensitive to a need, translates "free of grief" as "unblighted."

13. See Leach, *Culture and Communication,* 14 and 69–70, for this use of metonymy. After giving the example of the crown as a "sign for sovereignty," Leach concludes (14): "Very roughly . . . metonymy is where 'a part stands for the whole'."

14. Apollod. *Bibl.* 3.14.2; Steph. Byz., s.v. *Areios pagos*. The story was told by Hellanicus (fr. 1 in Jacoby, *FGrH* 3 B 41–42). See also Eur. *IT* 945–947; Dem. 23.66; Paus. 1.28.5.

15. Cf. Zeitlin, "The Dynamics of Misogyny," 159–160:

The solution moves to repair the female archetype which has been polarized at its extreme negative limit in response to its rejection and denigration. The solution also establishes marriage as the institution that controls sexuality and ensures fertility even as it serves to assert the inherent subordination of female to male. For female dominance is expressed paradigmatically by the mother-child relationship—concretely in the *Oresteia* by Iphigenia's death as the motive for the female's attack upon the male and generically by the natural dependency of the male child upon the adult female. Patriarchal marriage is paradigmatic of male dominance including the primacy of the father-son bond in patrilineal succession and the primacy of the male in political power.

Although I concur with this as a description of what happens at the court, what happens there is not a repair of the female archetype. The latter is not made whole but is maimed to leave only those parts essential for the continuation of male society—namely, the feminine. Clytemnestra, in fact, represents the whole archetype, since she embodies both the female and, in her Erinyes, the feminine.

16. F. Stoessl, *Die Trilogie bei Aischylos* (Baden: Rohrer, 1937), 46 and 226.

17. See Clytemnestra's injunction to the Erinyes (Aesch. *Eum.* 137–139): "You, blow your bloody breath upon him, waste him away with your smoke; with fire of your entrails, pursue him again and destroy him."

18. Aesch. *Eum.* 94–96.

19. For the prologue at Delphi see Taplin, *The Stagecraft of Aeschylus*, 362–376, esp. 368–369.

20. Aesch. *Eum.* 218 and 231.

21. Aesch. *Eum.* 430–435.

22. Aesch. *Eum.* 604–605.

23. Aesch. *Eum.* 606–608.

24. Aesch. *Eum.* 734–741.

25. For a review of the issue and various opinions see Michael Gargarin ("The Vote of Athena," *AJP* 96 [1975]: 121–127), who describes "Athena's vote as producing the tie verdict and thus acquitting Orestes" (127). Trials in the Areopagus were held before whatever number of jurors happened to be present. A tie vote in such circumstances was seen as the work of a god and

taken to indicate divine will for acquittal. The text gives us no reason to assume with many translators a jury of twelve. Twelve is a prejudice from the British and American systems of "bringing twelve good men into a box."

26. In this scene Aeschylus interpenetrates dramatic and contemporary events and, without breaking the illusion of the play, seems to be striving to create the feeling that jurors and audience are one. (Athena addresses the jury as "people of Attica" [*Eum.* 681]; how would the audience not see itself as included in that number?) The issue about to be voted upon by the jury on stage has been argued in topics familiar to the "jurors" of the audience. Everyone in the theater thus "participates" in the decision. The theory of embryology espoused by Apollo was known at Athens and was not so different from the common metaphor for *procreation,* that of the farmer plowing the furrows of his field. (See Arist. *Gen. An.* 763 b 30-35 for this theory, which is seriously asserted by Aeschylus. Vickers (*Towards Greek Tragedy,* 413-416) provides an excellent discussion of *Eum.* 658 ff. For *field* as metaphor see Aesch. *Sept.* 752-756 and Soph. *OT* 260 and 1497-1498). A few years before (c. 462/61 B.C.), the Athenians, in a move away from traditional aristocratic policy followed at the time by Cimon, turned from Sparta, their ally against the Persians, to join with the Spartans' archenemy, Argos. Athena's court itself, one of homicide, recalled the bitter strife of about the same period, when the actual court of the Areopagus was stripped of its political powers and its jurisdiction was restricted to murder and other religious matters. (For these events see Arist. *Ath. Pol.* 25 and 27.1; Plut. *Per.* 9.3-5; Ehrenberg, *From Solon to Socrates,* 208 and 211-213; G. E. M. de Ste. Croix, *The Origins of the Peloponnesian War* [London: Gerald Duckworth, 1972], 183-184; for political allusions in the *Eumenides* see K. J. Dover, "The Political Aspect of Aeschylus's *Eumenides,*" *JHS* 77 [1957]: 230-237.) Both alliance and reform were democratic measures and so presumably met with the approval of the majority of the audience. On stage they become founding events in the period of the beginnings of the Athenian polity. The balloting on stage, then, is equated with casting a decision on democracy and the city around the theater; the vote of condemnation is equated with a rejection of Athens and Athena.

27. Winnington-Ingram, "Clytemnestra and the Vote of Athena," 143.

28. Aesch. *Eum.* 778-787.

29. On the *epiklēros* see Lacey, *The Family in Classical Greece,* 139-145. Vernant ("Hestia-Hermès," 147) points to Hestia as the mythic model of the *epiklēros:*

> In the case of the institution of the *epiklēros,* the daughter of the
> house incarnates, even in marriage, the paternal hearth. Thus are found

reconciled in the person of the *epiklēros* the two aspects of Hestia, usually dissociated among mortals: the virgin daughter of the father; the woman, reservoir of life.

30. Martin P. Nilsson, *The Minoan-Mycenaean Religion and Its Survival in Greek Religion,* 2nd ed. (Lund: C. W. K. Gleerup, 1950), 483–501; B. C. Dietrich, *The Origins of Greek Religion* (Berlin: Walter de Gruyter, 1974), 154–158 and 181–183.

31. Harrison, "The Composition of the Amazonomachy on the Shield of Athena Parthenos," 125–126.

32. Ibid., 129.

33. The present analysis is confined to the shield of Athena Parthenos and makes no claims to include all meanings of the gorgon.

34. Eur. *Ion* 987–992. Euripides (994) represents the myth as being old, which, according to Ulrich von Wilamowitz-Moellendorff (*Euripides: Ion* [Berlin, Weidmannsche, 1926], 132–133), is an indication of its antiquity. It is also mentioned by Diodorus (3.70).

35. For the ideal of self-sufficiency (*autarcheia*) see André Aymard, "L'idée de travail dans la Grèce archaïque," *Journal de Psychologie normale et pathologique* 41 (1948): 19–45; Adkins, *Merit and Responsibility,* 226–232, esp. 231.

Bibliography

Adkins, Arthur W. H. *Merit and Responsibility: A Study in Greek Values*. Oxford: Oxford University Press, 1960.

Anderson, J. K. *Military Theory and Practice in the Age of Xenophon*. Berkeley and Los Angeles: University of California Press, 1970.

Bamberger, Joan. "The Myth of Matriarchy: Why Men Rule in Primitive Society." In *Woman, Culture, and Society*, edited by Michelle Zimbalist Rosaldo and Louise Lamphere, 263–80. Stanford: Stanford University Press, 1974.

Barrett, W. S. *Euripides: Hippolytus*. Oxford: Oxford University Press, 1964.

Barron, John P. "New Light on Old Walls: The Murals of the Theseion." *JHS* 92 (1972): 20–45.

Bennett, Florence Mary. *Religious Cults Associated with Amazons*. New York: AMS Press, 1967.

Boardman, John. *Athenian Black Figure Vases*. London: Thames and Hudson, 1974.

——. *Athenian Red Figure Vases: The Archaic Period*. London: Thames and Hudson, 1975.

Bothmer, Dietrich von. *Amazons in Greek Art*. Oxford: Oxford University Press, 1957.

Carlier-Détienne, Jeannie. "Les Amazones font la guerre et l'amour." *L'Ethnographie*, 1980–81, 11–33.

Connor, W. R. "Theseus in Classical Athens." In *Quest for Theseus*, edited by Anne G. Ward et al., 143–74. New York: Praeger, 1970.

Delcourt, Marie. *Hermaphrodite: Mythes et rites de la bisexualité dans l'antiquité classique*. Paris: Presses universitaires de France, 1958.

Denniston, John Dewar, and Denys Page. *Aeschylus: Agamemnon*. Oxford: Oxford University Press, 1957.

Detienne, Marcel. *The Gardens of Adonis: Spices in Greek Mythology*. Translated by Janet Lloyd. London: Harvester, 1977.

Deubner, Ludwig. *Attische Feste.* 1932. Hildesheim: Georg Olms, 1966.

DuBois, Page. *Centaurs and Amazons: Women in the Pre-History of the Great Chain of Being.* Ann Arbor: University of Michigan Press, 1982.

———. "On Horse/Men, Amazons, and Endogamy." *Arethusa* 12 (1979): 35–49.

Ehrenberg, Victor. *From Solon to Socrates: Greek History and Civilization during the Sixth and Fifth Centuries B.C.* 2nd ed. London: Methuen, 1973.

Farnell, Lewis R. *The Cults of the Greek States,* vol. 2. Oxford: Oxford University Press, 1896.

Feldman, Thalia. "Gorgo and the Origins of Fear." *Arion* 4 (1965): 484–94.

Ferguson, W. S. "The Salaminioi of Heptaphylai and Sounion." *Hesp.* 7 (1938): 1–74.

Fraenkel, E. *Aeschylus: Agamemnon.* 3 vols. Oxford: Oxford University Press, 1950.

Frazer, James George. *Apollodorus: The Library.* London and Cambridge, Mass.: William Heinemann and Harvard University Press, 1921.

Furtwängler, A. "Gorgones und Gorgo." In *Aüsfuhrliches Lexikon der griechischen and römischen Mythologie,* edited by W. H. Roscher, 1:1695–1727. Leipzig: B. G. Teubner, 1884–1890.

Harding, Phillip. "Atthis and Politeia." *Hist.* 26 (1977): 148–60.

Harrison, Evelyn B. "The Composi-tion of the Amazonomachy on the Shield of Athena Parthenos." *Hesp.* 35 (1966): 107–33.

Harrison, Jane Ellen. *Prolegomena to the Study of Greek Religion.* 3rd ed. Cambridge: Cambridge University Press, 1922.

Herington, C. J. *Athena Parthenos and Athena Polias: A Study in the Religion of Periclean Athens.* Manchester: Manchester University Press, 1955.

Herter, Hans. "Theseus." In *Realencyclopädie der classischen Altertumswissenschaft,* edited by A. Pauly, G. Wissowa, and W. Kroll, supplement vol. 13:1045–1238. Munich: Alfred Drukenmüller, 1973.

———. "Theseus der Athener." *Rh. Mus.* 88 (1939): 244–326.

———. "Theseus und Hippolytus." *Rh. Mus.* 89 (1940): 273–92.

Howe, Thalia Phillies. "The Origin and Function of the Gorgon-Head." *AJArch.* 58 (1954): 209–21.

Jacoby, Felix. *Die Fragmente der griechischen Historiker.* Vol. 1, *Genealogie und Mythographie. A, Vorrede. Text. Addenda. Konkordanz.* Leiden: E. L. Brill, 1957. Vol. 2, *Zeitgeschichte. A, Universalgeschichte und Hellenika.* Leiden: E. L. Brill, 1961. Vol. 3, *Geschichte von Staedten und Voelkern (Horographie und Ethnographie). B, Autoren ueber einzelne Staedte (Laender).* Leiden: E. L. Brill, 1950. *b (Supplement), A Commentary on the Ancient*

Historians of Athens. Leiden: E. L. Brill, 1954. *b II, Notes-Addenda-Corrigenda-Index*. Leiden: E. L. Brill, 1954.

Judeich, Walther. *Topographie von Athen*. Munich: C. H. Beck'sche, 1931.

Kennedy, George. *The Art of Persuasion in Greece*. Princeton: Princeton University Press, 1963.

Lacey, W. K. *The Family in Classical Greece*. London: Thames and Hudson, 1968.

Lattimore, Richmond. *Aeschylus I: Oresteia*. Chicago: University of Chicago Press, 1953.

Leach, Edmund. *Culture and Communication*. Cambridge: Cambridge University Press, 1976.

Lebeck, Anne. *The Oresteia: A Study in Language and Structure*. Washington, D.C.: Center for Hellenic Studies, 1971.

Liddell, Henry George, and Robert Scott. *A Greek-English Lexicon*. Edited by Henry Stuart Jones and Roderick McKenzie. 9th ed. Oxford: Oxford University Press, 1940.

Merck, Mandy. "The City's Achievements: The Patriotic Amazonomachy and Ancient Athens." In *Tearing the Veil*, edited by Susan Lipshitz, 95–115. London: Routledge and Kegan Paul, 1978.

Nauck, Augustus. *Tragicorum Graecorum Fragmenta*. 1889. Hildesheim: Georg Olsm, 1964.

Neumann, Erich. *The Great Mother: An Analysis of the Archetype*. Translated by Ralph Manheim. 2nd ed. Princeton: Princeton University Press, 1963.

Nilsson, Martin P. *Cults, Myths, Oracles, and Politics in Ancient Greece*. Lund: C. W. K. Gleerup, 1951.

———. *The Mycenaean Origin of Greek Mythology*. 1932. New York: W. W. Norton, 1963.

Parke, H. W. *Festivals of the Athenians*. London: Thames and Hudson, 1977.

Pembroke, Simon. "Women in Charge: The Function of Alternatives in Early Greek Tradition and the Ancient Idea of Matriarchy." *Journal of the Warburg and Courtauld Institutes* 30 (1967): 1–35.

Pomeroy, Sarah B. *Goddesses, Whores, Wives, and Slaves: Women in Classical Antiquity*. New York: Schocken Books, 1975.

Robert, Carl. *Die griechische Heldensage*. Vol. 2, *Die Nationalheroen*. 1921. Zurich: Weidmann, 1967.

Rosaldo, Michelle Zimbalist. "Women, Culture, and Society: A Theoretical Overview." In *Woman, Culture, and Society*, edited by Michelle Zimbalist Rosaldo and Louise Lamphere, 17–42.

Rosellini, Michèle, and Suzanne Saïd. "Usages de femmes et autres nomoi chez les 'sauvages' d'Hérodote: Essai de lecture structurale." *Annali della Scuola normale superiore di Pisa* 8 (1978): 949–1005.

Schroeder, Otto. *De laudibus Athenarum a poetis tragicis et ab oratoribus epidicticis excultis.* Göttingen: Officina Hubertiana, 1914.

Segal, Charles. "The Raw and the Cooked in Greek Literature: Structure, Values, Metaphor." *CJ* 69 (1974): 289–308.

———. *Tragedy and Civilization: An Interpretation of Sophocles.* Cambridge: Harvard University Press, 1981.

Slater, Philip E. *The Glory of Hera: Greek Mythology and the Greek Family.* Boston: Beacon, 1968.

Taplin, Oliver. *Greek Tragedy in Action.* Berkeley and Los Angeles: University of California Press, 1978.

———. *The Stagecraft of Aeschylus: The Dramatic Use of Exits and Entrances in Greek Tragedy.* Oxford: Oxford University Press, 1977.

Thompson, George. *The Oresteia of Aeschylus.* Amsterdam: Adolf M. Hakkert, 1966.

Tyrrell, Wm. Blake. "A View of the Amazons." *Classical Bulletin* 57 (1980): 1–5.

Vernant, Jean-Pierre. "Ambiguïté et renversement: Sur la structure énigmatique d'Œdipe-Roi'." In *Mythe et tragédie en Grèce ancienne*, by Jean-Pierre Vernant and Pierre Vidal-Naquet, 101–31. Paris: François Maspero, 1972.

———. "Hestia-Hermes. Sur l'expression religieuse de l'espace et du mouvement chez les Grecs." In *Mythe et pensée chez les Grecs,* 1:124–70. Paris: François Maspero, 1974.

Verrall, A. W. *The 'Eumenides' of Aeschylus.* London: Macmillan, 1908.

Vian, Francis. "La fonction guerrière dans la mythologie grecque." In *Problèmes de la guerre en Grèce ancienne,* edited by Jean-Pierre Vernant, 53–68. Paris: La Haye, 1968.

Vickers, Brian. *Towards Greek Tragedy: Drama, Myth, Society.* London: Longman, 1973.

Vidal-Naquet, Pierre. "Le chasseur noir et l'origine de l'éphébie athénienne." *Annales: Économies, Sociétés, Civilisations* 23 (1968): 947–64.

———. "Esclavage et gynécocratie dans la tradition, le mythe, l'utopie." In *Recherches sur les structures sociales dans l'antiquité classique,* 63–80. Paris: Centre National de la Recherche Scientifique, 1970.

———. "Les jeunes: Le cru, l'enfant grec et le cuit." In *Faire de l'histoire 3,* edited by Jacques le Goff and Pierre Nora, 137–68. Paris: Gallimard, 1974.

Walters, K. R. "Rhetoric as Ritual: The Semiotics of the Attic Funeral Oration." *Florilegium* 2 (1980): 1–27.

Webster, T. B. L. *Potter and Patron in Classical Athens.* London: Methuen, 1972.

Whallon, William. "The Serpent at the Breast." *TAPA* 89 (1958): 271–75.

Winnington-Ingram, R. P. "Clytemnestra and the Vote of Athena." *JHS* 68 (1948): 130–47.

Wolff, Hans Julius. "Marriage Law and Family Organization in Ancient Athens." *Traditio* 2 (1944): 43–95.

Wycherley, R. E. *The Athenian Agora III: Literary and Epigraphical Testimonia.* Princeton: J. J. Augustin Glückstadt, 1957.

———. *The Stones of Athens.* Princeton: Princeton University Press, 1978.

Young, D. C. C. "Gentler Medicines in the *Agamemnon.*" *CQ* 14 (1964): 1–23.

Zeitlin, Froma I. "The Dynamics of Misogyny: Myth and Mythmaking in the *Oresteia.*" *Arethusa* 11 (1978): 149–84.

———. "The Motif of the Corrupted Sacrifice in Aeschylus' *Oresteia.*" *TAPA* 96 (1965): 463–508.

Index

161